Acclaim for

The Curse of the Singles Table

"Hilarious, honest, and hopeful.... This book made me laugh out loud."

—*Lian Dolan,* The Satellite Sisters, *ABC Radio Networks*

"As someone who went dogsledding and camping—in Minnesota, in December—after a massive breakup, boy can I relate.... Schlosberg weathers her discontent—and yes, defrosts her cold spell—with wit and warmth."

—*Lynn Harris, author of* Miss Media *and* Breakup Girl to the Rescue!

THE CURSE *of the* SINGLES TABLE

A TRUE STORY OF 1001 NIGHTS WITHOUT SEX

SUZANNE SCHLOSBERG

WARNER BOOKS

NEW YORK   BOSTON

The identity of some of the persons referred to in this book and certain details about them, including all screen names, have been modified.

Warner Books
Time Warner Book Group
1271 Avenue of the Americas, New York, NY 10020
Visit our Web site at www.twbookmark.com.

Printed in the United States of America

First Printing: June 2004
10 9 8 7 6 5 4 3 2 1

Library of Congress Cataloging-in-Publication Data

Schlosberg, Suzanne.
    The curse of the singles table : a true story of 1001 nights without sex / Suzanne Schlosberg.
        p. cm.
    ISBN 0-446-69054-6
    1. Schlosberg, Suzanne. 2. Single women—Biography. 3. Man-woman relationships. 4. Celibacy—Humor. I. Title.
    HQ800.2.S35   2004
    306.81'53'092—dc22
                                                    2003024236

Book design and text composition by Nancy Singer Olaguera
Cover design by Brigid Pearson
Cover photo by Alan Powdrill/Taxi

To Nancy Kruh, a masterful editor

and remarkable friend

Acknowledgments

$\mathcal{I}$ owe more than I can express to Nancy Kruh (a.k.a. "Kate"), who insisted I write this book and helped me through it in countless ways. Right up there are my "other" Nancy, Nancy Gottesman, who had more than one finest moment, and Paul Spencer, my Epilogue Guy, who changed everything.

I'm grateful to Felicia Eth for working hard to sell this book and to Amy Einhorn for taking a chance on it and holding me to high standards.

I'm also indebted to everyone who lived through the Streak with me, who offered feedback on the manuscript, or both: Cristina Acosta, Colleen Dunn Bates, Teri Breuer, Daryn Eller, Amy Hutner, Ann Japenga, Jack Kearney, Richard Kim, Rebecca Kotch, Matt Levinson, Randee Motzkin, Richard Motzkin, Natalie Nathgall, Liz Neporent, Bennett Ross, Rick Scott, Allan St. Pierre, Robyn Polashuk, Margie Schwartz, Sarah Bowen Shea, Nora Slaff, Chris Sorrentino, Tracy Sturman, Dana Sullivan, Bren Unger, and Sarah Wilke. I must single out Julie Solo for her exceptionally careful read and invaluable suggestions.

Finally, I want to thank my parents; my grandparents; my sister, Jen; her husband, John; my cousin Michelle; and her husband, Kevin, for their support, their love, and their endless supply of great material.

Contents

The Streak:
The Dark Ages

Love is the answer—but while you're waiting for the answer, sex raises some pretty good questions.

—Woody Allen

1

~~~~~~

One Thousand Days

I could tell you that I came to the most remote corner of Arctic Russia because of an interest in life on the tundra in the post-Soviet era. Except it wouldn't be true. The reason I'm here is that I have gone one thousand forty-four days without sex.

Let me clarify: I did not come to Provideniya to get laid. That would be like traveling to North Dakota for Ethiopian food. There are maybe forty single guys in this town, and it appears that the majority are border guards wearing the type of oversized sunglasses last seen on *Starsky and Hutch*. Not a good look, really.

The truth is, I came to Provideniya—a near ghost town of crumbling concrete with no cafes, no hotels, not even hot running water—because it seemed like the perfect place to commemorate my One Thousand Days. My own personal New Millennium.

The fact that I have been stranded here for a week

seems especially appropriate. The fact that I don't really want to leave comes as a bit of a surprise.

I can't recall exactly when I started counting, but at some point, back home in Los Angeles, I did some calculations and determined that I was closing in on a historic milestone. One thousand days, in case you're doing some calculations of your own, is ninety-two days shy of three years. It is just thirty-six days shorter than the duration of the Kennedy administration. Other than my parents' former housekeeper, Esperanza, an ex-nun from El Salvador, I do not know anyone under the age of seventy who has even approached this record.

With no prospects in sight, I am, at age thirty-four, becoming the Cal Ripken of celibacy.

Now, I'm sure you're wondering how I got into this predicament. Do I look like Freddy Krueger? Do I dress like Barbara Bush? Am I too picky? Too bitchy? Too shy? Do I have agoraphobia? Chlamydia? Really bad foot fungus?

Good questions, all of them. Questions that I have, at one time or another, mulled over. Questions that members of my family ask frequently and loudly at our Jewish-holiday gatherings.

The short answer to all of these questions is no. Or, as they say here in Provideniya, *nyet*.

I suppose I could have sex. In fact, just last month, through my Internet dating service, I received the following e-mail from a twenty-one-year-old bicycle messenger: "I would like to spend a night with a wonderful woman. I am young but I am mature. I am French, also. I love pleasure, exchange of energy! What about you?"

The thing is, most consenting adults can find sex, if they're willing to go to bed with someone they're not especially attracted to or fond of. But here's the other thing: Yes, I'm looking for sex, but I'd like something more, too. At the very least, I'd like a little mutual desirability. I'd like the tiniest spark. And I'd like a guy who can utter the phrase "I feel" in a context other than "I feel like eating at Burger King."

Don't get the wrong idea: I am not all that virtuous. I'm certainly not saving myself for Mr. Right. I'd be perfectly amenable to taking Mr. Remote Possibility for a test drive. But somehow, despite my valiant efforts over one thousand days, even he doesn't seem to have made an appearance. As a consequence, I've been left in a state of sexual deprivation that I previously thought impossible. What's it like to go without sex this long? Well, let's just say that unlike Cal Ripken when he was riding his streak, nobody's cheering, least of all me.

During my epic dry spell, I've been out with so many guys that I have developed a system of dating strategies complex enough to warrant doctoral study. I have vowed to broaden my search, to try harder. I've vowed not to try at all and just "let it happen." I've tried to appear more available and less assertive. I've tried to appear less available and more assertive. I've done just about everything but lower my standards or give up completely, because the truth is, I still have hope. Greater miracles have occurred. Remember the South American rugby players who survived a plane crash in the Andes in the dead of winter? If they could live for ten weeks on toothpaste and the flesh of their deceased teammates and still manage to walk out of the mountains alive, surely I can navigate my way out of singlehood, no?

Still, as I stand by and watch almost everyone I know get paired off, I do wonder what's going on. Is this bad luck? Is it fate? Is this predicament of my own making? I've never believed there is just one perfect match out there for me—there are probably dozens, if not hundreds. But why do they all seem to be in a witness protection program?

Some months ago, it became evident that my countless efforts, large and small, would not keep me from reaching One Thousand Days. Short of a miracle to throw me off course, I was headed straight toward this ignoble benchmark.

Clearly, an event of this magnitude called for some sort of tribute (to myself, of course, for my remarkable endurance). I briefly considered a solo trip to Death Valley, but commemorating my dry spell in the desert . . . I don't know, the concept just seemed unimaginative. A few friends suggested I go somewhere fabulous, like Tahiti or the Italian Riviera or Jackson Hole, Wyoming. But fabulousness was clearly not what the situation warranted. Fabulous is for your honeymoon, not your impersonation of the Virgin Mary.

The worst advice came from Kate, a friend who's appointed herself my own personal airbag, ready to deploy whenever she thinks I'm about to get hurt. "Go pamper yourself at a spa!" she insisted. "Blow lots of money on beauty treatments!" It was obvious that Kate had never been to a spa and had only read about them in perky women's magazines.

I, on the other hand, have been to several spas, having been sent on assignment, as it happens, by the various perky women's magazines that I write for. I can tell you that the suffering usually begins with a facial. You are led into a dark room by a pale, stout Bulgarian named Magda, who wears a white lab coat and uses a giant magnifying glass to inspect your pores under the blinding glare of a floodlight that could do double duty in police interrogations. She then demands to know what cleansing, toning, and moisturizing products you use—and why you have so little regard for your skin as to have purchased any of the products you just mentioned (if you could think of any). Suddenly you are engulfed in steam, and Magda gouges her sharpened thumbnails into your nasal cartilage, sighing as she extracts blackheads visible only through her electron microscope. Then she grabs a spiked pizza slicer and rolls it all over your face.

It's one thing to have endured one thousand days without sex. It would be like pouring lemon juice on a canker sore to commemorate the occasion by visiting a spa.

Pampering was out. But what was the alternative? I was searching the Internet one night when I hit upon a trip that seemed to strike the perfect tone: the Arctic Ocean Ride of Pain. It was an eleven-day mountain-biking and camping trek along the unpaved Dalton Highway, the most remote road in the United States, stretching 450 miles from Fairbanks, Alaska, up to a town called—I loved this part—Deadhorse. Temperatures would likely be near freezing, and there would be no showers, no toilets, and except for the world's northernmost truck stop at mile 174, no services at all. "Let it not be said that we didn't warn you!" the tour company's Web site offered. I should mention that I'm an avid cyclist, so this trek seemed to offer the proper amount of torture without the risk of death.

I did more research and discovered that I could cap off the Ride of Pain with a two-day side trip to Provideniya, a town 6,000 miles from Moscow but just an hour by prop plane from Nome, across the Bering Strait. I looked at the world map on my office wall. Russia, an enormous, orange blob, appeared to have a lot in common with my celibacy streak: It looked bleak and endless. It seemed like my kind of place.

Now, you may be wondering: What's the difference between spa pain and Arctic pain? It's all in the expectations. If you sign up for something that sounds fantastic but turns out to be dreadful, you end up feeling ripped off and bummed out. But if you go in expecting misery, you can only be pleasantly surprised.

Today is day seven of my two-day "side trip" to Provideniya. Back in Nome, the tour company operator had mentioned that planes can't fly out of Provideniya when it's foggy. What she didn't happen to mention is that (1) it's almost always foggy here, (2) foggy or clear, the airport is closed on weekends, and (3) even on weekdays when the weather is clear, airport power outages can still keep you grounded.

Every morning, my fellow inmates and I gather around our apartment window and gaze out at the fog, wondering when the requisite stars will align to spring us from this joint. The others in the group—two retired couples from Texas and a shy, forty-ish software engineer from Seattle—are becoming increasingly anxious to get out of here. Last night when Yuri, our local guide, mentioned that a group of Japanese scientists once got stranded in Provideniya for a month, the whole lot of them looked positively stricken.

But I could hardly contain my good humor because, personally, I'm in no hurry to go anywhere. I'm still basking in the glory of my arm-wrestling victory over a Russian teenager the other day at the rec center. (Hey, he started it.)

I've got dozens more American slang expressions to teach Yuri—"You're bullshitting me" is his new favorite—and I'm still perfecting the Scrabble board I made out of notebook paper and duct tape. I've got stuff going on.

Besides, as I look at the rusted tanks and decaying boats outside, it occurs to me that I've been given a rare and unexpected opportunity. For the first time in ages, there is absolutely nothing I can do about my streak—no online dating services to pore over, no setups engineered by well-meaning friends, no strategies to implement simply because they're so wacky they've got to work. Without any pressure or distractions and only time on my hands, maybe I can finally get to the bottom of things. Maybe I can figure out why, over the past one thousand forty-four days, I managed to get so far off track. How did I go from being a person who has sex to being a person who thinks an abandoned military outpost in Arctic Russia is a really great place to vacation?

If I can figure that out, then maybe I can figure out a way to put an end to the Streak, and begin the rest of my life.

2

~~~~~~

The Curse of the Singles Table

*O*f course, it's not just about the sex. Sooner or later, I'd like the sex to come packaged with a wedding ring.

Why get married? For love, companionship, children, for someone to help pay the mortgage and field the telemarketing calls—all the usual reasons. But when you're in your thirties, the prospect of marriage offers one particularly alluring perk: the end to insufferable singlehood.

Not that singlehood, as a concept, is entirely dismal. At certain times of life, being unattached is actually quite a blessing. In your early twenties, singlehood allows you to be spontaneous and madcap—to put your belongings in storage and bicycle across the country, to have sex with your coworkers in your Trooper in the company parking lot. At this point, marriage is a concept as alien and disconcerting as a colonoscopy.

Late-twenties singlehood isn't a bad deal, either. A couple of your friends have gotten engaged, but you're not hearing any ticking clocks, and you're feeling free to sleep with cute guys you're certain would never be husband material. If your family starts nagging you, you just pack up your Trooper and move to a new city.

But then there's over-thirty singlehood, which is basically like being sent to the Gulag. This fate becomes very clear every time you attend a wedding and are seated at the Singles Table.

In your twenties, the Singles Table is not a bad place to be. Sure, you're disappointed that you didn't have a date for the wedding, but you look upon your singleness as a common and temporary condition, like the flu. In fact, when you glance over at the Married Twenty-Five-Year-Olds Table, you're quite glad you're not sitting there, especially since you'd be wearing pearls and other items of jewelry and clothing that would suggest a premature transformation into your mother. You're sure all the Married Twenty-Five-Year-Olds made a grievous error—that in ten years they'll wake up wondering why the stranger in their bed prefers flipping channels to having sex and how much money they'll need to spend on couples therapy to bring their marriage out of its vegetative state.

In your twenties, you take your place at the Singles Table with optimism. You know there will be a decent crop of available guys at your table, and it's not inconceivable that one of them might become your next fling, or maybe even your next boyfriend. At the very least, you'll have someone to dance with.

In your thirties, the Singles Table is a very different place. Now, the population of this table resembles that of a war-torn nation: women, children, and sickly men. Typically there are not enough bona fide singles to fill an entire table, since all the people you sat with in your twenties have found their mates. So the definition of "single" is stretched to include engaged couples, eleven-year-old nephews of the groom, and paunchy second cousins from Detroit who manage their father's drywall business.

In your thirties, you dread taking your place at the Singles Table. Your singleness has started to feel like something more serious than the flu, something chronic, painful, and obscure—like diverticulitis. Deep down you know you haven't done anything to cause your condition, but you know that other people suspect it's your fault, and in your worst moments you start to wonder if they're right.

In your thirties, the conversation at the Singles Table goes through distinct phases. In the introduction phase, everyone behaves as if they are seated at any ordinary table. Conversation is along the lines of, "So, are you friends with the bride or the groom?" or "How long have you known Stacy and Steve?" Everyone takes turns telling their story— "Joan's uncle Charles is my mom's cousin's husband" or "Scott and I were fraternity brothers" and so on. In this phase, the dialogue is very similar, I imagine, to the conversation that goes on at all the other tables. For a good, solid ten minutes, you cling to the illusion that you are just like everyone else.

But then the music starts, and you're suddenly reminded that your tiny, tablecloth-covered island is a world apart. At first, you try to talk over the music, ignoring the fact that, ten yards away, two hundred people have flooded the dance floor. You try to act as if this is a wonderful opportunity to continue the fascinating conversation you began during the introduction phase. While the DJ blasts "Play that Funky Music, White Boy," you find yourself screaming across the Singles Table, "So, how many employees work in your division? Has the company always been based in St. Louis?"

At some point, the music becomes too loud and your situation too conspicuous (all of the tables except the Longtime Housekeeper and Elderly Distant Relatives Table have now emptied onto the dance floor), and you are forced to either flee to the bathroom or ask the second cousin from Detroit to dance, since he is far too meek, short, inept, or uninterested to think of asking you. So you and the second cousin venture to the edge of the dance floor and engage in some quasi-robotic movements without making eye contact—without really moving, actually. You pray that there will not be any slow songs and that the food will be served very, very soon.

Usually, sitting at the Singles Table is an indignity you endure in private. Sure, you're in a room with a few hundred other people, but they're all preoccupied, fawning over the bride and the table decorations, and your fellow singles are a nonissue because tomorrow they'll be off to Detroit or the sixth grade. When your mother calls for a wedding report, you can just say, "The flowers were beautiful" and "The rabbi was in top form" and so on. Nobody has to know.

But then there are times when the Singles Table ordeal is exacerbated by the fact that you have to endure it in front of your family. This happened to me recently at the wedding of two family friends, Marnie and Mike. My parents, my grandparents, my aunt and uncle, my sister and her husband, and my cousin and her husband were seated at one table. I was seated about thirty feet away, at the Singles Table.

Actually, at this particular wedding, the indignities began before the seating arrangements were even revealed. I drove to the affair with my cousin and her husband, whose unspoken function in the family is to accompany me to events where everyone else has a date. Once, they even insisted on bringing me to a Valentine's Day dinner, a thoughtful gesture that turned into a debacle when the three of us showed up at a restaurant that only had tables for two. We ended up at a seedy Thai joint seated in a booth.

Upon arriving at the synagogue, I promptly ran into my parents. My mother could not stop raving about how thin and gorgeous I looked, which is her usual attempt to over-compensate for the fact that I am dateless. The longer I am single, the thinner and more gorgeous I become, according to my mother. By the time I hit forty, I may well turn into Julia Roberts.

I will admit that I was fairly fetching that evening, thanks to a slimming black dress and velvet jacket that my father had bought for me on a recent shopping expedition. It is true: I am thirty-four years old and my father is dress-ing me. There are two explanations for this:

(1) Nobody in the family trusted me to show up at the wedding dressed appropriately ("appropriate," in my fam-ily, means new, expensive, and fabulous). Their instincts were correct. Left to my own devices, I would have done a cost/benefit analysis—Is it worth spending four hundred dollars for an event unlikely to yield a single prospective boyfriend?—and pulled a black suit from my closet. If my parents wanted to see me in a new outfit, they would have to buy it for me.

Which brings me to (2). I have neither the patience nor the talent to shop for dress clothes on my own, a deficiency I seem to have inherited from my mother. Left to her own devices, Mother favors knee-length Bermuda shorts with sweaters and tights. She's a whiz at analyzing the P/E ratios of technology stocks, but send her to an upscale clothing store and she's like Bambi lost in midtown Manhattan.

My younger sister, Jennifer, is an experimental artist turned graphic and interior designer with a superior fashion sense. Her personal preference is to go for shock value—low-cut, fluorescent-orange blouses and pumps that are impossibly high and pointy—but she has done a stellar job as a personal shopper for my more sedate tastes. However, Jen and I were not on speaking terms as Marnie and Mike's wedding approached, an unfortunate and complicated situation dating back to her own recent wedding. Alas, my father was the only available candidate for the job.

He was, I should add, an outstanding candidate. A fine-art dealer and connoisseur of flowers, furniture, and apple martinis, my father was born to shop. He wears Panama hats and wingtip shoes and mustard-colored herringbone blazers with a handkerchief peeking out of the breast pocket. When he travels, he often gets upgraded to first class simply because he looks the part. My father does not know how to throw a football or operate a power saw, but he is a genius when it comes to matching dresses, scarves, and wraps. In less than one hour, my father had found me the perfect outfit for Marnie and Mike's wedding. I was grateful. Better to be dateless and gorgeous than dateless and drab.

As I sat in the synagogue trying to stay awake during yet another explanation of the Jewish wedding rituals, the rabbi's words suddenly caught my attention. Reading from a poem, he announced that marriage joins two people whose lives, previously, were "worthless, without purpose." Well, well, well. How marvelous, I thought, for Marnie and Mike to have evaded this miserable fate. Bravo for them! But what about the rest of us worthless, purposeless masses sitting out here?

After the ceremony, we filed into the hallway to pick up our place cards. That's when I discovered I'd been banished to the Singles Table. As I walked over to my place, my family waving to me in dismay, I felt like a criminal defendant being taken into custody after bail had been denied.

One by one throughout the evening, my family stopped by to commiserate or lobby for my release. "We'll just grab a chair and squeeze you in!" one cousin suggested. Jen's husband, John, surveyed my fellow singles, the usual slim pickings, and shook his head. "Man, you've gotta blow this joint," he said before being abruptly summoned to push Grandpa Julius to the men's room in his wheelchair. My aunt implored me to join the family. "You belong with us," she said.

But did I? The ten people at my family's table were all coupled up. Wouldn't that make me the eleventh wheel? Plus, the cramped quarters at the family table would have made my predicament even more obvious. I feared the conversation that might follow and thought back to my cousin's wedding, when Grandma Honey cornered me in the restroom and demanded to know why, at age thirty-one, I had no marriage prospects. "Where do you fit into all this?" she asked, before heading out the door and onto the stage for a lengthy speech in which she proclaimed, "At least one of my grandchildren will be married before I'm dead!"

I know Grandma Honey (a childhood nickname for Hannah) means well. She just wants me to be happy, and obviously, she has decided that marriage is the shortest route to that destination. Which, in itself, is fascinating to me since marriage is the very institution that has made her life miserable. "Living hell," "nightmare," and "Sometimes I'd rather be dead" are just a few of the terms she uses when speaking about her sixty-six years of wedlock to Grandpa Julius, a cantankerous retired business mogul.

In the early years, according to reliable sources, my grandmother's marriage consisted primarily of planning and executing lavish parties to impress my grandfather's associates in the coat-manufacturing industry. Otherwise, Grandpa was blessedly out of her hair, off barking orders at his salesmen or intimidating his business associates in Europe. These days Grandma is stuck with him and his tirades twenty-four hours a day, since she can't see well enough to drive and wouldn't leave him alone anyway, for fear that he would forget to take his blood pressure medicine and drop dead of a stroke, thus leaving her with unbearable guilt. Now that Grandma is ninety, her marriage entails fixing Grandpa breakfast, administering eye drops for his glaucoma, and living in a retirement-home suite that is hotter than Guatemala in August. (Grandpa is always cold but refuses to wear sweaters, so he blasts the heat instead.) And still, Grandma Honey insists that I get married.

My other grandma, Ruth, held marriage in equal reverence, even though she was divorced twice herself and did not approve of ninety percent of all spousal choices made by anybody related to her. To put this in context, I should mention that Grandma Ruth disapproved of pretty much everything, especially exercise, politics, credit cards, four-door sedans, and Israeli accents. Still, when I'd visit for our weekly Scrabble game, her first question to me was always, "So when are you going to get married?" I would feign momentary shock and say, "Oh my God, I can't *believe* I forgot to tell you! I'm getting married on Saturday! I hope you have something to wear!"

As Grandma Ruth grew older and weaker, she couldn't remember whether "agria" was a legitimate Scrabble play (the word, which means "severe pustular eruption," is indeed fair game, as Grandma herself had taught me), but she always remembered to pester me about finding a husband. When, at age eighty-nine, she became so frail she could barely sit up, her greetings were reduced to a single word: "Married?"

Grandma's dead now, but that hasn't really helped the situation, since I have several dozen other relatives standing by to remind me of my single state.

Now, you may wonder why, given the marital train wrecks previously described, I still aspire to utter the words "my husband." One reason is that unlike my grandmothers, who married very young, I've milked singlehood for all it's worth. Another reason I remain hopeful is my parents. For more than three decades, they've had the kind of love affair that could be accompanied by the soundtrack to *When Harry Met Sally.*

Romance? My father will light six pairs of antique candlesticks in their bedroom and serve my mother sherry from a crystal decanter. He loves to make dinner an event, moving their table for two to the den fireplace, to the side yard near the rosebushes, or to the bedroom, within view of the saucer magnolia tree.

Respect and admiration? Sometimes my father will call me from his car phone just to say, "You should have seen your mother at the Rosenfelds' party last night. She was just exquisite in her green dress and diamond earrings, and she didn't look a bit tired, even though she drove Grandma to the urologist and Grandpa to the dermatologist and spent four hours updating their finances on the computer. I hope my next wife is half as capable and brilliant and gorgeous."

Of course, there will be no second wife. My father is only joking. He is almost always joking, except when it comes to professing his love for my mother.

My mother is no less effusive. Her calls to me from the car phone are testimonials about my father's sense of style, his flair for adventure, and his ability to sell expensive paintings to people who did not even realize they were in the market for art. "He's a miracle worker," she'll say. "He's one in a billion."

My parents' marital compatibility is all the more remarkable considering the only thing they really have in common is that they despise all feature films except those starring Meryl Streep.

My father is an optimist, certain that his next art exhibition will be an unprecedented success. My mother is the pessimist, just as sure the whole endeavor will drive them to bankruptcy. My mother lives in a constant state of assessment: Has she chosen the right homeowner's insurance? The correct toner cartridge for her printer? The proper ratio of onion bagels to egg bagels? The only issue my father takes the time to assess is whether the bar in the den is low on vodka.

And yet, somehow, my parents get along marvelously. Watching them is really quite magical. Naturally, they want the same for me. They will not say as much—thank goodness—but I can sense their longing. They want it so badly that my father has even taken to reading the personal ads in *The Jewish Journal*. Not long ago he came across a thirty-eight-year-old writer whom he felt was perfect for me. He was so sure that he secretly called the writer on my behalf. Dad was forced to admit this egregious behavior to me when it turned out that the prospective date he'd selected was a former coworker of mine, a guy who was clearly as uninterested in me as I was in him.

So perhaps you can understand why I was not leaping toward the family table at Marnie and Mike's wedding. At least there was a place designated just for me at the Singles Table. Unfortunately, it was next to a guy who spent most of the evening stalking a woman seated on the other side of the room. That left an empty space between me and the other nonrelative single guy. I expended a great deal of effort leaning across the empty space and feigning interest in the fact that his on-again, off-again girlfriend plays fullback on an all-women's contact football team. About halfway through the meal I gave up on the conversation and focused instead on eating the table-decoration grapes in a symmetrical pattern, so the centerpieces would not be ruined by the bare stems.

By the time we finished the chicken and asparagus, the Singles Table had been largely abandoned, a common yet mysterious phenomenon. It's not clear where everyone goes, and I've never taken the time to investigate. I suppose the engaged couples get swallowed up on the dance floor, and the eleven-year-olds try to scam some booze from the bar. My usual strategy is to leave the event altogether, so as to avoid participation in the ultimate indignity: the bouquet toss.

This loathsome tradition has been eliminated from most weddings I attend these days, since the brides and grooms are typically in their thirties and have no single friends left to participate. However, as I learned from my friend Cara's wedding, you just never know when this custom, like a bad credit report, will resurface and ambush you.

The best thing that happened to me at Cara's wedding was that, while walking to the garden for the postceremony photo shoot, I tripped down the concrete steps and sprained my ankle. The immediate humiliation, including the wedding coordinator's frantic pursuit of an ice pack, was mitigated by the fact that I now had the perfect excuse to leave the party early. I took full advantage of my injury, limping out the door as soon as dinner was over.

The next day I learned that, after I left, I had been paged by someone at the microphone onstage. If I'd been there, I would certainly have ventured up, on the assumption that I had lost my keys or wallet. As it turned out, I'd been summoned for the bouquet toss, which apparently was supposed to have involved three people: the two flower girls and me.

I didn't know if Marnie would be having a bouquet toss, and I didn't want to find out. With the Singles Table now empty, I wandered back over to my family's table, where my grandfather and I discussed the recent increase in his dosage of congestive heart failure medication. "I've got to go to the john all the goddamn time," he said. Fearing that a trip to the men's room was imminent and would involve me piloting the wheelchair, I decided I'd served my time at this wedding. I grabbed my cousin and her husband, and we split.

When you're single in your thirties, you are often overcome by this urge to flee. But you're not just running away—from the latest airborne flower bouquet or baby shower or New Year's Eve bash. You're running toward something—or at least that's what you tell yourself as you buy your plane ticket.

Every time my birthday comes around or a friend gets

engaged or the holiday season appears on the horizon, my impulse is the same: I pull out my *Rand McNally Road Atlas* or log onto a bargain travel Web site. For just $599, I discover, I can go to Malta for a week, airfare and hotel included! I don't even know where Malta is, but for a split second, I feel a surge of optimism. Maybe I'll meet my next boyfriend on the beach in Malta! (But wait, does Malta have beaches? Or is that Yalta?) I feel certain that the more remote the destination and the more taxing the trip, the more possibilities await me.

Fleeing gives you more than a sense of relief, more than a means to distract yourself while everyone else is opening a joint checking account. It gives you hope that you can find a way out of your predicament.

But perhaps I'm getting ahead of myself. I daresay, the day Cal Ripken trotted out to third base in 1982, he had no idea it was the start of a record-setting, 2,632-consecutive-game streak. I was similarly oblivious to what lay ahead. In fact, up until the first day of my One Thousand Days, sex had pretty much been like Häagen-Dazs. It wasn't something I had every day, but I figured it would always be available.

B.C.E.

(Before the Celibacy Era)

Some things are better than sex, and some things are worse, but there's nothing exactly like it.

—W. C. Fields

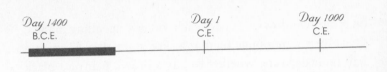

3

Life with Sex

$\mathcal{T}$he most notable thing to come out of my sex life with Bradley, the predominant boyfriend of my early twenties, was that I memorized the official birds of all the *M* states: Maine, Maryland, Massachusetts, Minnesota, Mississippi, Missouri, and Montana. Bradley had a map of the United States posted above his futon, and it featured alphabetized columns listing the fifty states and their corresponding birds. Whenever we'd have sex, a monotonous event that took place about once a week in his cat-hair-coated studio apartment, I would inevitably end up positioned in front of the *M*-state column. To pass the time, I would bone up, so to speak, on my birds. "Maine: Chickadee," I'd say to myself, as we went at it. "Montana: Western Meadowlark."

As a couple, Bradley and I had all the appeal of a chopped-liver-and-jelly sandwich. During our three years together, we constantly complained about each other's music, each other's apartments (him: "Could your bedroom be any more cavelike?"; me: "Could you maybe put *blinds* on your windows?"), and each other's spending habits. Once we got in a huge fight at a shoe store after he spent a half hour debating whether to buy a brown pair or a black pair of forty-dollar dress shoes. When I suggested that he throw caution to the wind and buy both, he accused me of being Imelda Marcos incarnate. "I only have one pair of feet!" he snapped as I stormed out of the store.

At this point, you may be wondering why I was with Bradley at all, let alone for a period lasting longer than most Hollywood marriages. I have thought about this long and hard and have settled on an explanation: cluelessness. The early twenties, at least as I experienced them, are not particularly conducive to making deeply considered decisions. At this point, you are little more than an amoeba with a credit-card balance. Your obtuseness applies to pretty much every aspect of life, whether it's your behavior at the office, your roommate-selection process, or the guys you hop into bed (or the back seat of a Trooper) with.

Granted, there are exceptions to this rule. There are people who make all the right moves from birth and have decided on a career, a spouse, and a city to settle in by the time they're old enough to vote. But since neither I nor any of my friends ever fit into that category, I have to assume these people either are (1) freaks of nature, or (2) living in countries with limited job opportunities and arranged marriages.

More typically, it seems, the early twenties are exemplified by a tendency toward being monumentally impulsive or dense. Certainly this explains how I ended up with a career writing articles like "Flat Abs by July!" and "A Firm Butt in 3 Moves!" Basically: I didn't get my year-end raise at the newspaper I worked for because, according to my boss, I frequently rolled my eyes at assignments I didn't like. I quit in a huff and took the first job that came along, a position at a women's fitness magazine favored by readers who consider cellulite to be only slightly less horrifying than the threat of global nuclear warfare. (I enjoy exercise as much as the next person—probably more so—and I'm hardly procellulite, but surely there are obsessions worthier than the pursuit of sculpted glutes.)

An ample supply of impulsiveness also explains why I shared a rental house for two years with a girl I met at a bowling alley, who brought along a mangy mutt that did nothing but hump the couch and relieve himself on my bedroom carpet. To a certain extent, it also explains Bradley, the last in a series of starter boyfriends that began in college.

When it came to sex, I was late off the blocks, but that's what tends to happen when you spend six years sequestered in an all-girls prep school, especially one so strict that you're sent to detention for wearing sneakers instead of regulation loafers. By my first year at college, though, I was determined to catch up. And so I began a mutually obsessive flirtation with a button-down upperclassman in my Spanish class. He was smart and dorky in a cute kind of way, and I cornered him for our first kiss in an empty hallway outside our language lab.

I was the one who brought up sex, a few months later, but he kept begging off. When we finally ended up fumbling through my farewell to virginity in his off-campus apartment, I did make a mental note that he appeared to be showing the same amount of excitement toward my breasts as one might show toward, say, a pair of moldy tomatoes. But I had nothing to compare our encounters to, so it never occurred to me that we might be engaged in the worst sex ever experienced by two consenting adults. Nor did it occur to me—or to him, until several years later—that he was gay.

When I moved on to my second boyfriend, Eric, a sorta-cute, sorta-dorky writer on the campus paper, I told him that sex, in my view, was like step aerobics—an inexplicably popular activity that was, in reality, nothing more than a succession of variations on the same uninspiring moves. Luckily, he realized that I just hadn't had the right instructor. He unhooked my bra with one hand, unzipped my jeans with the other, and moments later, I made a surprising and life-changing discovery: Sex was fun!

I mark this as the official moment when my Life With Sex began, and it seemed infinitely superior to the alternative. Over the next few years and sexual partners, I stumbled onto several more conclusions. First of all, there seemed to be distinct categories of sex. For me, these consisted of: bad sex with guys who turned out to be gay (see Boyfriend No. 1); good sex with nice guys worthy of a fleeting coed crush (see Boyfriend No. 2); weird, regrettable sex with guys who would never be more than friends; and fantastic sex with smart, hunky guys who would inevitably dump you.

My impulsive forays into so-called "friendly" sex were especially disastrous. On paper, this would seem to be the perfect outlet for carnal lust. You're between boyfriends. You want sex. And you're put off by the bar scene. Why not sleep with your favorite office pal sitting a few cubicles away? He's decent-looking, and there's no danger of hurt feelings, since you both know you lack the chemistry to go the distance. What could go wrong?

But then you start kissing, and you realize there was a reason you'd never mentally undressed the guy: You're not attracted to him. At all. You go through with the sex anyway—you'd already agreed to it and you're long overdue—but the pleasure instantly gives way to a torrent of horror and embarrassment. Why couldn't you have just played Yahtzee? When it's all over, you both pretend nothing has changed—you might even believe it at the time. But soon you realize that, in a matter of a few libidinous moments, you have managed to destroy a year, maybe two years, maybe even five years, of friendship. The really amazing thing is that, within months, you reenact the whole sorry tale with yet another male friend.

Eventually, of course, you land another boyfriend (just in the nick of time, since you're now running short on people to go to the movies with). Maybe this time you hit the jackpot and end up with a chiseled, charming guy you adore. Even better, you get to revel in the fact that a guy so chiseled and charming seems to adore you. My own chiseled charmer was a sportswriter named Dave who wore a baseball cap, drove a Datsun 280ZX, and called me "darlin'." He had smooth skin and a repertoire of smooth lines ("You look good, you taste good, you feel good, you smell good . . ."). Dave did have his limitations—most notably his inability to confine himself to a single girlfriend, which I didn't figure out until after we'd broken up. But during the year Dave and I dated, my sexual learning curve was phenomenal. I would like to say this was because he tenderly and patiently showed me the ropes, but really it was because one day he suggested that I go read a sex handbook and learn the basics. I was so mortified that I actually did.

When Dave finally dumped me (with an excuse that I no longer recall), I was crushed, devastated, pulverized—and it didn't help that he had a new girlfriend within minutes of our breakup. Ultimately, I emerged with a new philosophy about boyfriends: Great-looking guys are trouble. Too much emphasis is placed on appearance, and only naïve women think that the charms of romance and great sex are integral to a lasting relationship. In fact, I decided, it's just the opposite: Infatuation signals inevitable doom. Sure, you need an element of attraction, but wild sexual passion is not a plus. Better to have a relationship built on a mutual interest, such as television crime dramas.

So perhaps now you can understand why I hung on to Bradley. By the time we'd been dating for a couple years, I was so convinced that Mr. Right was just a fantasy that I contented myself with Mr. Pretty Okay Except for the Weird Cheapness and Boring Sex. Ignoring a truckload of evidence to the contrary, I somehow persuaded myself that Bradley and I were actually good for each other. After all, we were both writers who enjoyed bicycling and working out at the gym. What a miracle! What an uncanny coincidence! What kismet! In my amoebalike wisdom, I managed to conclude that it was doubtful I'd ever find someone more suitable. The fact that Bradley and I didn't much like each other seemed incidental.

Although Bradley was perpetually overcome with inertia—over the course of thirty-two months together he never managed to wash his car or buy a pillow for my side of the futon—he did, thank goodness, finally muster the motivation to dump me. He was thirty-three and wise enough to realize we were a lousy match. I was twenty-six and very sad. For about ten minutes.

And then it dawned on me: I was free! For the first time, I realized I was way too young to entertain the concept of settling for either a passionless relationship or a dead-end job. I had been handed a second chance, and I was not going to screw up again. Figuring my career could survive a hiatus and my life needed a jump start, I quit my job, broke my lease, and signed up for a seven-week bicycle tour across the country, from Los Angeles to Orlando, Florida. I was done memorizing state birds. I wanted to see the states.

That's where this story really begins.

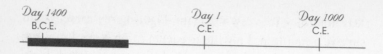

Day 1400
B.C.E.

Day 1
C.E.

Day 1000
C.E.

4

Good Cop/Bad Cop

$\mathscr{I}$t was on the third day of the bike trek that I noticed, among our group of seventy cyclists, a guy with short salt-and-pepper hair, beefy triceps, and the most endearing way of applying sunblock—carelessly slathering it all over his face rather than preciously dabbing it, like Bradley used to. I learned his name was Alec and he was a cop from Berkeley, California. He looked a bit like Bruce Willis circa *Die Hard,* and I could not take my eyes off him. In fact, I was developing neck strain from keeping him under constant surveillance.

Alec seemed to have noticed me, too, as he would mysteriously appear next to my bicycle each morning just when I was ready to take off. We quickly became riding partners.

Even though he was forty-four, which seemed to me ludicrously ancient for a guy I was lusting after, Alec had this kidlike loopiness that made me forget he had graduated high school the year I was born. We'd be pedaling alongside an alfalfa field, and he'd flag down a farmer for a ride in his tractor. He'd ask a trucker parked at a rest stop if we could tour the cab of his eighteen-wheeler. In New Mexico, we heard about an eighty-eight-year-old woman who lived alone on a ranch with no electricity and was known to castrate her own bulls. "Man, we gotta meet this broad," Alec said, and so we hitched a ride to her ranch with a local. (We'd have cycled there except it was apparently unsafe for strangers to show up unannounced. "Mrs. Taylor's a good shot," our driver warned.)

Alec seemed to have a lot of good qualities, but one stood out: his ability to be happy all the time without annoying the shit out of me. Not that I prefer a sour state, but honestly, you can stand only so much perkiness before you've got to wonder, Who left the door unlocked and let in the Brady Bunch? Alec never complained about anything—not his job, not the mosquitoes that feasted on us through our Lycra, not even his mother. "My ma—she's good people," he'd say. Considering that my family's mantras were "The traffic was a nightmare" and "The brisket was at least two hours undercooked," I found Alec's good cheer refreshing, if a bit strange.

Also strange: Even though Alec and I spent nearly every waking hour together for those first three weeks, he never so much as brushed up against me. In my experience, guys who were interested in you made it obvious, with moves ranging from a gentle touch on the back to the more straightforward "Do you want to grab a pizza and watch the fight?" Guys who were not interested made their feelings clear, too, either by politely keeping their distance or by flicking you away like a piece of lint on their sweater. I had never been sent such mixed signals.

But I was no longer the Suzanne who just let things

rock along; the new me was more proactive. So one morning at a truck stop in West Texas, I kissed Alec on the cheek before darting off to the restroom. When I returned, so nervous I was dizzy, he acted as if nothing had happened.

The proactive me suddenly made a quick exit, and I got back on my bike, also pretending nothing out of the ordinary had occurred. The next two days were excruciating, and I began to wonder: Had I only imagined I'd kissed him? Or could he be so dense that he didn't realize what my kiss meant? Or could he be too embarrassed to tell me straight-out that he wasn't interested? Why was he making this so difficult?

Now, I've never thought a girl should have to sit passively and wait for the guy to make the first move, a system that seems about as flawed and outdated as the electoral college. Yet somehow, just like the electoral college, it still hangs around, and I'd never been much on trying to buck it. So I resorted to the next-best thing: manipulative plotting and scheming. I erected my tent next to Alec's one certain destination: the men's restroom. I enlisted one of my new friends to mention my name in front of Alec to see if she could detect any flickers of interest—a half-step, I admit, above junior-high note passing. But I got nowhere, and the suspense was keeping me up at night. Two days later, on a sweltering afternoon toward the end of a ninety-mile ride, Alec and I stopped to rest on a park bench. Sunblock was dripping down my face. My braid had split apart, and stray hairs were popping out of my helmet. I was hot and sweaty, and suddenly I had lost all patience with my situation. "So," I blurted out, "are you interested in me or *not*?"

Alec smiled and said, "Of course I am," and gave me a real kiss.

"Then why," I asked as soon as our lips unlocked, "did you ignore my kiss the other day?" Alec mumbled something about being wary of "entanglements," a comment I chose to ignore. I realize now that when it came to red flags, I was utterly color-blind.

I moved into Alec's tent that night, at a campsite somewhere outside of Galveston. Once I'd turned on the faucet, he began gushing affection. For the next four weeks cycling became something we did in between having sex—much better sex than I'd had before. In fact, with Alec I discovered a whole new category: fantastic sex with smart, hunky guys who are more than just chiseled charmers. I felt like we were in one of those romantic-comedy montage sequences set to a Harry Connick score. Cut to Suzanne and Alec having sex in a barn in Texas! Cut to them doing it at a Louisiana cemetery! Cut to them fooling around on the grounds of an antebellum mansion in Mississippi! On one of the final mornings of the trip, at a motel in Florida, Alec rolled over in bed and said what no guy had ever told me before: "I think I'm in love with you." I was so grateful that Bradley had cut me loose. I didn't think my life could possibly get any better.

By the end of the trip, I'd decided to take another bold step: move to Berkeley. I'd always been dubious of women who dropped their lives to follow their hearts, but now, in my state of euphoria, I understood perfectly. I was so sure things with Alec would work out that I didn't even feel like I was taking a risk. Besides, there was nothing waiting for me in L.A.—no job, no apartment, no boyfriend back home. Alec did happen to mention that he had no intention of ever getting married, but I just assumed he hadn't met the right woman. Plus, I was having way too much fun to worry about the future. When you're twenty-seven, marriage can still be something you're going to get around to later, like reading *Anna Karenina*.

From Florida, I called my family back in L.A. to report the big news. Perhaps you're wondering what they had to say about my moving four hundred miles from home for a police sergeant eighteen years older than me—a cop whose lifetime experience with Judaism consisted of the night he worked security at a Yom Kippur service. Well, "mazel tov" was not it.

My mother announced I'd just dropped "a ton of bricks" on her head. Grandma Honey told me flat out; "I'm placing a big red warning light on your shoulder. You're making the biggest mistake of your life." She kept referring to Alec as "that motorcycle cop," despite the fact that he did not actually ride a motorcycle. Who knew *CHiPs* had so deeply penetrated the psyche of the octogenarian set?

Not that I expected my family to send me a Harry and David fruit basket, but I didn't predict they'd act as if I were running off with Mike Tyson. Since my parents had sensed my boredom with Bradley—my dad had said, "Congratulations!" upon learning of our breakup—I thought that given my obvious enthusiasm for Alec, they might actually be happy for me. But then, I failed to grasp one of the fundamental truisms about parents: They want the best for you, but only if it doesn't involve sex with a forty-four-year-old cop.

Their disapproval shocked me and upset me and only steeled my resolve to prove them wrong. The more my family objected to Alec and dismissed my campaign material ("But he's in amazing shape for forty-four!" "But he's young at heart and has never been married!" "But he owns six rental properties and has traveled to sixty-six countries!"), the more I hoped things would work out between us, if only to deprive Grandma Honey of the pleasure of saying "I told you so."

Shortly after the trip, I drove a U-Haul up to Berkeley and took an apartment near the police department. I'd gladly have moved in with Alec but wasn't bothered when he balked. My more rational side conceded that it's probably not a good idea to live with a guy you've known for less than a full TV season.

Despite my family's dire predictions, my new life got off to a stellar start. I was relieved to discover Alec was the same person in reality that he had been during our seven-week *Fantasy Island* on wheels. I was sure Grandma Honey was going to have to eat her words.

Alec and I settled into a comfortable daily rhythm. I worked on freelance fitness stories from home—articles like "Fight Fat and Win!" suddenly seemed more palatable now that I was not writing them in a cubicle—while Alec sat in a police car waiting to bust dope dealers. Every few hours he'd call to see whether I was writing or whether I was pretending to write while watching the O. J. Simpson trial. We'd often meet for a gym workout on his break or for dinner while he was on duty, but since he worked until 2 A.M., sex usually had to wait until his days off. I had no complaints. We successfully made that transition from first-blush infatuation, where you feel like two human suction cups, to the point where you can actually go a full forty-eight hours without a desperate life-or-death urge to hop into bed.

Alec and I seemed especially in sync when we went on vacation. Since he had two decades of travel on me and was on a mission to visit one hundred countries, he'd already been to most places in the world that I had heard of. So we climbed sand dunes in Namibia. We snorkeled off the Micronesian island of Yap. We drove Nevada's Extraterrestrial Highway. There was nothing tedious about being with Alec.

Except, after a while, listening to his commentary on the subject of marriage. At first, I was amused by Alec's views on wedlock, which could basically be summarized as, "What am I, freakin' stupid?" I'd chuckle when Alec would identify his fellow cops by how many times they'd been divorced: "Zuckman—two ex-wives, two ex-houses, three ex-kids" or "Wagner—has to work four years past retirement to make up for the percentage of his pension going to his ex."

I was even amused by Alec's affinity for country-music videos about breaking up. His favorite was Blackhawk's "Goodbye Says It All," which featured a woman on a houseboat smashing her husband's TV set with his golf clubs. Every time the video would play on Country Music Television, Alec would leap off the sofa like a football fan watching his team score a touchdown. "Check this one out!" he'd shout, waving me over. "This is the best video ever! Look, she's about to throw his TV overboard!"

But after two years, the act got old. I began to see that Alec's antimarriage shtick wasn't a shtick. For reasons I could never completely unearth, he really was fanatically opposed to marriage. While I wasn't paying attention, he had managed to freeze our relationship in the "ain't we got fun" phase, and it had never progressed an inch farther.

Now, if you're a levelheaded single woman who, on occasion, fantasizes about that one true love, you know you're going to have to put up with certain idiosyncracies, like an unhealthy attachment to a maroon velour sweater or an obsession with video games like Madden Football '96. But you also know there are certain things that qualify as deal breakers. For instance, the wife he forgot to divorce. Or his membership in a satanic cult. Or perhaps worst of all, his complete and utter rejection of the noble institution known as marriage.

Whenever I approached the subject of Our Future Together, Alec seemed to instinctively pull away as if I were poking him with a sharp stick. "What do you mean by 'future'?"

"You know *us*—you and me? The two people who spent twenty-seven hours driving to Arkansas so you could relive the glory of your high-school paper route?"

It wasn't that I'd already chosen my bridesmaids. And even at the time I realized there were other complications to Alec's suitability as a husband, such as our age difference and his opposition to having children. But if Alec truly wasn't open to even the most infinitesimal possibility of marriage, I had to ask myself, What was I hanging around for?

Perhaps even more to the point, I had to ask my friends. Not that I've ever been short of my own ideas, but when you're dealing with the big issues, you can't have too much feedback. You also can't have too many hands to pull you back from the brink of doing something really stupid. Just as the president has his Cabinet, you have to have a few choice girlfriends as your go-to advisors—sort of your own personal cabinet. The size of mine has fluctuated at times, but usually it consists of about a half dozen friends that I've collected since college. They're a diverse bunch, in various stages of singlehood, couplehood, and parenthood, and each has her own war story and advice expertise. But they've all gained their cabinet-level positions because they have one thing in common: They're not shy about offering an opinion.

When I began expressing my quandary about Alec to them, the consensus seemed to be that I shouldn't be so tormented. "Be grateful you found someone you can have so much fun with," said Ann, a friend in her mid forties whose fifteen-year marriage has endured its share of ups and downs. A writer who specializes in philosophical essays, she has emerged over the years as my secretary of uncommon wisdom. "Life is about compromises," she told me. "Can't you just figure out a way to make it work?"

Even Nancy, my most practical cabinet member, came down on the side of romance. "It's obvious that you love the guy," she said. "You can't just throw that away." Nancy had spent three years listening to me whine about Bradley when we shared a cubicle at the fitness magazine, and I'd long since grown to depend on her no-bullshit sensibilities. She's never been afraid to tell me what I don't want to hear—one certain mark of a great friend. On the other hand, Nancy's own personal life has been soap-opera caliber. Married briefly in her twenties, she was now in a nine-year, on-again, off-again relationship with the father of her three-year-old, and once, just to hedge her bets, she'd cautioned me, "Always do the opposite of what I tell you."

Kate, the human airbag, told me to stop worrying about making a decision about Alec. Over the years, she'd worn a groove in her therapist's couch dealing with an assortment of "issues" and crises, including a failed marriage that involved a now ex-best-friend as a third party. She now channeled her considerable energy into trying to spare her loyal friends any variety of emotional pain. "If the time comes that you need to move on, you'll do it," she said.

Still, my doubts kept nagging at me. Sure, this relationship was better than the one I'd had with Bradley. But then

again, *Lethal Weapon 2* was better than *Lethal Weapon*, and
how much was that saying? Deep down I knew that Alec and
I weren't really merging our lives; we only had frequent inter-
sections. I suspected that would never change, and I didn't
want to repeat the Bradley scenario, clutching to a going-
nowhere relationship just because leaving seemed too scary.

Of course, relationships can't remain idle indefinitely,
and if they don't go forward, they start rolling in reverse,
which is what happened to us. Inevitably, the sex began to
fizzle and Alec's idea of emotional intimacy became curling
up in front of the TV with me and watching *Road Test
Magazine* rate the new Ford F-150. That spontaneous "I
think I'm in love with you" back in Florida never made any
return appearances. I decided it was, in retrospect, one of
those "excited utterances" the DAs are always arguing
about on *Law & Order*: a true statement, sure, but one
"arising out of a startling occasion" (great sex for twenty-
eight straight days?) and "not the result of deliberate reflection by the declarant."

Nearly three years into our relationship, Alec and I took
a trip to Italy. One day the train operators went on strike, so
we walked to the bus station and chose a destination at random: Montepulciano, a medieval town in Tuscany. As we
sat in the bus, winding past rustic farmhouses and sun-
splashed vineyards, I burst into tears. Here we were, in one
of the world's most romantic spots, and I felt like I might as
well have been there with my pizza-delivery guy.

Okay, remember when Red Sox first baseman Bill
Buckner let Mookie Wilson's ground ball roll through his legs
in the sixth game of the 1986 World Series, handing the Mets
a victory? Well, that's about as deftly as Alec handled my
tears. He didn't assure me that he loved me or, for that mat-

ter, even that he was happy to be in Italy with me. Instead he said, "Geez, man, why do you always want to know where the relationship is *going*? Can't you just enjoy the ride?"

But I couldn't. Not when it felt like an amusement-park ride—something that kept ending up right where it had started. It wasn't that I had any regrets, but I knew, at age thirty, that any more time I did give him would be a waste. Although I said nothing more on our bus ride, I knew this series was over. What Alec wanted was a playmate. What I wanted was evidence we were headed somewhere besides destinations that not even Arthur Frommer could find on a map.

Sadly, it was time to move on. I knew I was going to have to be the one to initiate the break, since Alec seemed so content with the way things were. And just like the way I'd started this whole thing with, "So, are you interested in me or *not*?" I knew there wasn't a smooth way to end it, either. It was pretty clear which one of us was going to plunge into depression and which one of us was going to shrug and park himself in front of Country Music Television's "Top 20 Video Countdown." The mere thought of splitting up made me teary. Actually doing it seemed unfathomable. So I decided to deal with the trauma the best way I knew how: by delaying it.

To minimize the magnitude of my inevitable meltdown, I sought to devise a postbreakup coping strategy even before the split. If I simply announced, "We're through" and went home to my apartment, I'd likely spend the next six months sobbing and/or obsessively watching Court TV. What I needed was something to distract me from wallowing in the fact that I'd invested three years in a guy with the emotional depth of a dust mite. I needed a plan.

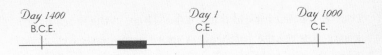

Day 1400
B.C.E.

Day 1
C.E.

Day 1000
C.E.

5

Lollapasuza

*A*s fantasies go, the Perfect Breakup isn't quite up there with the Perfect Wedding, the Perfect Vacation, or in the case of my father, the Perfect Cashmere Turtleneck. Still, I think anyone who's ever been in a doomed relationship—which I assume is pretty much everyone short of the pope and the Olsen twins—has conjured up a best-case breakup scenario to help soften the inevitable blow.

The Perfect Breakup, of course, involves no sobbing or hurling of breakable objects or potshots like "By the way, half the time I was faking it!" No, the ideal split involves the mutual arrival at the sad but mature conclusion that going your separate ways is for the best. It involves soothing assurances like "You'll always have a place in my heart" and "I'm a much better person for having known you" and "I wouldn't trade our time together for anything in the world."

In the dream breakup, you spend one last night together, and the sex is gentle, wistful, and amazing because, of course, it's just for old times' sake. Then, in the morning, he kisses you on the forehead (a more genuine sign of affection, in my opinion, than the perfunctory cheek kiss), thanks you for all the good times, and sends you off with best wishes for a happy life. On his way out, he even helps you pack up the U-Haul.

That was my fantasy. The reality would remain to be seen because I was, for the time being, ensconced in that spineless phase of partnership known as Lame-Duck Girlfriend. This is when you amble along for a couple of months privately attempting to get used to the idea that, however it will happen, the split is inevitable. During this phase, you spend half your time plotting a breakup that will make him beg you to stay—a plot that involves serious consideration over which outfit you'll wear for the big announcement, hopefully one that will remind him of all the sex he'll be giving up. The other half of your time is spent either (1) searching for evidence that you'd be a fool to leave him or (2) indulging in the irrational hope that there's still time for him to undergo a complete personality transplant.

Keeping my secret from Alec wasn't hard to pull off. He had remarkably perceptive powers when it came to catching crooks, but he seemed to be oblivious to the fact that his girlfriend was slowly checking out of the relationship. I did weather some guilt about scheming behind his back; I wasn't exactly being the model of honest and open communication that I'd longed for him to be. But I didn't feel *that* guilty. How bad can you feel about leaving someone who thinks he's got it made with a passport, a pension, and a pickup truck with a super cab?

Still, being a lame-duck girlfriend is no holiday. There's

some relief in knowing you've made a decision, but there's also the stress of living a double life. You have to act as if everything's normal—"Hi, honey, did you arrest anyone today?"—when, in reality, your world is collapsing.

The best coping strategy, I found, was focusing on where I would go post-Alec. In my mind, there was no question I'd have to move away. I had no reason to stay in Berkeley. I had no roots there and not that many friends, and once the cashier at our favorite Mexican joint figured out Alec and I had broken up, I knew I'd probably stop getting free (a.k.a. "police price") sodas. Plus, I'd constantly worry about running into Alec, which would only dredge up painful memories. It's not so tough to dodge an ex-boyfriend who's an accountant or a plumber, but just try to avoid a guy who cruises your neighborhood in a patrol car.

Where, though, would my new home be? Nebraska? Alaska? Mauritius? The magazines I freelanced for didn't care where I lived, as long as I had Internet access, so I basically had the entire world to choose from—a world that seemed a lot bigger to me than before I'd met Alec. It was a strange position to be in: I could wipe the slate clean, starting over in a whole new town with a whole new life. Yet I had no good reason to settle in any one place, nor did I have any idea what that new life would be. I felt both liberated and adrift.

I knew I needed to narrow my choices, so I started by jotting down my main criteria: clean air, minimal traffic, affordable rent, dry weather, a well-equipped gym, and hilly roads for cycling.

This meant L.A. was definitely out. Given the opportunity to live anyplace on earth, why choose a giant, smog-filled parking lot? Also, I didn't think I could stomach giving my family the satisfaction of my moving home. Even though Alec was about to become my ex-boyfriend, I was still annoyed that they'd never warmed to him. My grandparents had never even uttered his name, acting for three years as if I had moved to Berkeley for grad school.

Besides, what I wanted was radical change. Glancing at my list of criteria, I could see it was leading me away from the big city. Maybe it was time to see if I could make it on my own in a smaller community, like Mary Tyler Moore in reverse.

Gradually, I began to visualize my new life. I'd be so busy getting acquainted with this friendly new place—finding the best mom-and-pop bakery, learning that Thursday is meatloaf night at the corner diner—that I wouldn't have time to despair over the breakup. I relished the idea of landing in a spot where I would have no memories, no history, no ties— a place where I'd meet lots of new people, something I'd done little of in Berkeley. I think it's a truism: You always make more friends during periods of singleness. When you're part of a couple, it's so easy to tune other people out.

A small town also seemed like a good way to maximize my odds of finding the right guy. He wouldn't be stuck in traffic, and I wouldn't be overshadowed by liposuctioned blondes with gravity-defying breasts.

Feeling sad, nervous, and excited—usually all at once— I threw myself into the process of finding a new home. No more moves on a whim. This time, I was determined to think things through.

My one concession to the Schlosberg clan was confining my search to the American West, just a plane flight away from our endless series of family gatherings. So I descended on the public library, determined to read every guidebook on any town between the Colorado border and the Pacific Ocean. I learned the average January temperature in Spokane, the median two-bedroom rental price in Flagstaff, and the number of movie theaters in Billings, Montana. I discovered there were 563 yearly auto thefts in Albuquerque and 450 Jews in all of Idaho—about the same number residing in my grandparents' assisted-living complex in L.A. (The shortage of Jews did give me pause— would I be able to find a good bagel?—but at this point, I wasn't ruling anything out.)

As usual, I polled my half dozen cabinet members, but I also cast a wider net, surveying a variety of other friends. Basically, no one was any help.

"Boulder rules!" one said.

"Boulder bites," said another.

One friend lobbied for Portland, where she'd gone to college, although she later admitted she'd once succumbed to UV light therapy to treat depression brought on by sixty-seven consecutive days of rain. A friend from New York City glanced at my list of criteria—dry weather, hills, the West, a small community—and somehow came up with . . . Indianapolis.

My plan was to narrow my list of prospects to five, then embark on a tour. I would spend a few days in each town acting like a resident—loitering in the bookstores, evaluating the lattes, working out at the gyms.

Yet I sensed there was still something missing from my plan. If this was going to be a life-changing journey, shouldn't it sound like one? I concluded that what my trip needed was an official name. One friend suggested "Tour de Schlosberg," but that seemed trite. Another suggested

"SchlosAid," but that made me sound like a beleaguered hog farmer. Ultimately, I went with my friend Liz's idea: Lollapasuza. I considered printing T-shirts, but no sponsors surfaced.

With my research complete and the Lollapasuza tour dates set, there was one thing left to do. I had to actually break up with Alec.

Choosing when to break up is sort of like deciding when to schedule your next Pap smear: You just keep wanting to put it off. You'll drum up any number of excuses, like "It's too close to New Year's Eve" or "It's too soon after his birthday." And if you're stuck in one of those nonholiday stretches on the calendar, you'll use a rationalization like "I can't do it today because I still have to assemble my Micronesia photo album, and if I wait until after we break up, I'll be too much of a wreck to look at the pictures and it'll never get done."

But eventually you just have to brace yourself and take the plunge. So I finally picked out what I thought would be the right moment: the drive back from our fourth annual Death Ride.

The Death Ride is a one-day event held each year near Lake Tahoe, Nevada, that involves bicycling 130 miles over five mountain passes with sixteen thousand feet of elevation gain. In lay terms, this means "something you might want to try in a car." But for Alec and me and three thousand other people who didn't seem to mind paying fifty bucks for a day of suffering, the Death Ride somehow qualified as fun—a 4 A.M. breakfast, a 5:15 start, then twelve or so hours on the bike, depending on how much we'd trained, how long we lingered at the food stops, and whether we encountered rain, hail, raging wind, or scorching heat. Afterward, Alec and I would refuel on lamb and tongue stew at a family-style Basque restaurant and reflect on what a wonderful time we'd just had.

My friend Kate, ever trying to save me from myself, thought I had a screw loose for doing the Death Ride even once, let alone repeatedly, let alone the day before splitting up with Alec. "You want to torture yourself even more by topping it all off with a breakup?" she said incredulously. "Do you really need to take 'Death Ride' literally?"

She had a point, but the timing just seemed right to me. Our relationship had practically started with the Death Ride, which was just two months after we'd met. There was a symmetry to ending it with the ride, too. "Besides," I told Kate, "I already paid my entry fee, and they serve really great ice cream sandwiches at the top of the last pass."

When the ride finally came, and we began cycling out that morning, I felt tense and sad, knowing that, short of a miracle, this would be our last Death Ride together. To keep myself from falling apart, I focused hard on pedaling up the mountain passes. Alec had a sinus infection and was blowing out green gunk virtually the entire day but, as usual, finished looking like he'd gone for a twenty-minute jog. I was perfectly healthy but, as usual, looked like I'd spent, well, twelve hours on the bike.

After a restless night (both of us were too tired for sex—a good thing, since I'd have felt guilty even entertaining the thought of "for old times' sake"), I woke up the next morning determined to go through with my plan. As we drove away from Lake Tahoe in Alec's Jeep, my heart was pounding. I turned down the volume on the country music station and said, in a more cheerful manner than was warranted, "So, I think it's time for me to go." It seemed clear, I explained, that we weren't going to get married and since that's what I wanted for my life, I had no choice but to leave. In a few weeks, I told him, I'd be driving around the West to find a new home.

Now, I admit I was hoping against hope that Alec would say, "Wait, you can't go! You're the best thing that ever happened to me! Let's take a trip to Uzbekistan!"

Instead, he just shook his head and, expressing neither surprise nor disappointment, said, "Man, you'll never find anyone like me again."

Good, I thought to myself. *I'll find someone better,* even though, at that moment, I wasn't so sure I would.

True to form, Alec didn't ask me how long I'd been planning our breakup or where I was considering moving or how I felt. He basically acted as if I'd said, "So, I think it's time for me to go . . . to the dentist." We talked about our sore quadriceps and his phlegm and whether his lieutenant would take early retirement. His nonreaction to my big news confirmed that I was doing the right thing. But that didn't keep a part of me from still wanting him to ask me to stay.

"I'll call you tomorrow," Alec said as he dropped me off. But he didn't. We saw each other just once after that, at the gym. I was on the StairMaster reading *Outrage: The Five Reasons Why O. J. Simpson Got Away with Murder* when I saw him walking toward me. I was mature, I told myself as I pressed harder on each step. We'd had a civilized breakup, and now we were just going to exchange pleasantries.

"Hi," Alec said, and I promptly burst into tears. As usual, he had no clue how to handle it.

"Hey, I never made any promises," he said, shaking his head as he walked away.

I shut the book, hopped off the StairMaster, and made a mad dash for the door.

The night before I left town, I paged Alec. I suppose I was still hoping he'd leave the door open to some later reconciliation—or at least offer some Alec-ized form of "You'll always have a place in my heart" (perhaps: "Well, good to know ya"). But he never phoned back. So much for the Perfect Breakup. Clearly, it had been a ludicrous fantasy. I'd been so preoccupied daydreaming about what I wanted Alec to say that I'd avoided imagining what I knew he would say. Naturally, a meltdown ensued, but in between spontaneous crying jags I managed to throw myself into completing the planning of Lollapasuza.

Suffice it to say, my family knew none of this. My news filter winnowed all the breaking developments down to a brief story about going on a road trip with a friend who was recovering from a recent divorce. This would explain why Alec wasn't with me (not that they wouldn't be rejoicing over that), while sending a subtle signal that "recently divorced" may be even less desirable than "never married."

And so early one Tuesday I packed up my Trooper and hit the road. As I merged onto the interstate I already felt my blues turn a couple shades lighter. After months of indecision and dread over breaking up, I'd done it, and now I was finally headed somewhere. In just a couple weeks, I'd know where I would be starting my new life.

The first stop on my tour was Ashland, a town of twenty thousand in southern Oregon known for its year-round Shakespeare festival. I ruled it out immediately. Too many New Age bookstores. Too many wind chimes. Too much arugula. Not enough Office Depots.

Two days later I meandered over the Cascade Mountains

and pulled into Bend, a cheerful, sunny Oregon ski town of thirty-five thousand. I wandered around the charming Westside, inhaling the pine-scented air and surveying the craftsman-style cottages, the bicycle shops, the homey break-fast cafes. I lounged on a comfy couch in a coffeehouse, nib-bling on a just-baked oatmeal bar and reading the collage of posters that advertised acoustic music at the downtown pizza joint and a series of free outdoor concerts. I was getting good vibes. I liked the sense of community, the lack of pretense, and the fact that pretty much everyone, young or old, was wearing a fleece vest. But there seemed to be something more at work.

And then it struck me: my hair. Until that point, I'd been having what you could call a bad hair life. In Los Angeles, I'd walked around for years with a thick mass of unruly brown curls. In the Bay Area dampness, the situa-tion had worsened—my hair was a wild, frizzy mess more accurately described in terms of width than length.

But the bone-dry air of Bend had worked a miracle. It was as if, after thirty years coiled up in knots, my hair had let out a huge sigh of relief. It was soft. Flowing. Vertical. I saun-tered through the downtown park smiling, my hair bouncing like a Breck girl's. What magic, I wondered, could you find in a place where you looked your best without even trying?

My visit happened to coincide with Bend's monthly Jewish service, held in the basement of the Methodist church. I'd learned about the service while conducting demographic research on the Internet. On a lark, I had typed in "Jews" and "Bend," figuring the search would be about as fruitful as punching in, say, "big horn sheep" and "Mall of America." But up popped the Web site of the Jewish Community of Central Oregon, a loose-knit group of about seventy-five families—enough to support periodic services but not a synagogue or rabbi. I called the contact phone number and spoke to a friendly attorney named Steve. When I asked what it was like to be Jewish in a town that didn't even have a deli, he invited me to the service.

It's not that I was looking for spiritual renewal. Nor was I necessarily on the hunt for a Jewish boyfriend. If that had been the case, Lollapasuza would have been a tour of law offices, orthopedic practices, and commercial real estate offices in L.A., Chicago, and Manhattan. I just figured that mingling with the Jews would be an easy way to make friends, the way Denver Broncos fans who've moved out of state meet up at sports bars to watch the games.

At the Methodist church I found a fleece-wearing congregation sitting on folding chairs, reading from photocopied prayer books, and listening to a rabbi imported from Portland for the occasion. After the service, a half dozen people gave me their phone numbers in case I had more questions about Bend. So this was what small-town life was like. I hadn't been in town two days and I was already popular!

Bend had cast its spell on me, and after just two days, I could see myself settling down there. Still, I was determined not to make any snap decisions. So according to plan, I took off for Boise, which, for reasons I can no longer recall, was a trendy place to live in the late nineties. There I met up with two friends of a friend who were perhaps the oddest couple in all of Idaho: a tall, bald, soft-spoken, fiftyish literature professor named Jack and his high-strung, thirty-year-old Tunisian boyfriend, Raouf, who sported a buzz cut and an NYPD T-shirt. They treated me like a visiting dignitary, escorting me on an extensive tour of the city.

Jack and Raouf were most excited about taking me to the Western Idaho State Fair, where I paid a visit to an enormously pregnant Tarot card reader named Marta. Clearly, I was at a turning point in my life; perhaps Marta could offer some guidance.

"So where am I going to move?" I asked as Marta, seemingly in one motion, grabbed my fifteen bucks and flipped over some cards.

"East," she said confidently.

Whether she meant eastern Idaho or, say, Newark, was unclear. I then asked Marta whether she saw a new boyfriend in my future. She indicated she was having some sort of labor pains and waved me off. Considering her shaky performance up to that point, I decided not to read too much into her hasty departure, so I caught up with Jack and Raouf at the exhibit of giant cucumbers.

I realized Boise wasn't for me and left a day early to cover the 350 miles to Salt Lake City. With so many new people and places to absorb in less than two weeks, I was managing to keep my fixation on the breakup to a minimum. But every so often—on days like this one when I drove long stretches of empty highway—I'd suddenly start weeping. (It didn't help that Brooks and Dunn's "You're Gonna Miss Me When I'm Gone" was one of the big hits on country radio at the time.) There's something about a good cry that seems to trigger bouts of temporary amnesia. In this altered state, all I could remember were Alec's dimples and the adorable way he'd say, "Are ya working hard?" every time he'd call in from a stakeout. Completely forgotten was his approach to Valentine's Day, which was essentially, "Couldn't you just write yourself a card and I'll sign it?"

Soon, I'd find myself slipping into some light self-flagel-lation: Yeah, maybe he was an oaf, but at least he'd been *my* oaf. Sure, he had his weak moments, but who said I was per-fect? Maybe all we needed was a little more time. Maybe I could have figured out a way to make it work. Maybe if I hadn't been so demanding, so impatient, so narrow-minded. Maybe . . . maybe everything was my fault!

It was usually around this point in the misery process that I'd return to my senses, wipe away the tears, and renew my resolve to find a guy for whom February 14 signaled flowers and affection, not the annual running of the Daytona 500.

Salt Lake City, the most metropolitan stop on Lollapasuza, turned out to be a congested mess of freeway detours covered by a blanket of smog. Soon it began to drizzle, and my hair started to frizz, so I went on to Reno. After checking into a budget motel and working out at World Gym, I headed over to the synagogue, where I found the rabbi at her desk. I explained that I was looking to make a fresh start after a painful breakup, didn't know any-one in town, and was soliciting opinions on whether I should move to Reno.

"Don't come here," she warned. "Reno is not a good place to be single."

Now it's not as if I were some kind of celebrity, but I figured she'd pretty much be doing backflips at the prospect of increasing the city's minuscule Jewish population by one.

And so Lollapasuza was ending on an unexpected note: I had been rejected by the rabbi of Reno. The next day I drove back to collect my belongings with a sense of accom-plishment. I was headed for Bend, a place that was exactly what I wanted. My months of careful planning had paid off!

I called my family to report the news, hoping that by throwing enough new information at them at once—the breakup, the move, this new town I was certain they'd never heard of—they'd be too overwhelmed to process it all and criticize my decision.

"Bent?" my sister said. "You're moving to Bent, Oregon?"

"No," I said. "*Bend*. With a *d*. As in 'duh.'"

"Bend?" my dad said. "Like you bend an elbow?"

The news was evoking the desired impact. I had them off balance. But as I began describing my new idyllic home, my mother cut to the chase.

"Are there any single people there?" she demanded to know.

"Of *course* there are single people," I replied, irritated that she would ask even as I realized I had no idea.

Since most of my friends had known about Lollapasuza, I was hoping for a more positive response from them, but mostly what I got was, "What are you, fucking insane?" They began placing bets on how long I would survive, most of them wagering that I would not outlast the annual renewal date on my new gym membership.

Nancy gave me a double dose of straight talk. Now was the time for me to return home to familiar surroundings, she said, not to isolate myself in some random town—especially one that was three hours and one giant mountain range (the Cascades) from the nearest big city (Portland). But then again, this advice was coming from a woman who had been renting the same apartment for eighteen years.

"You don't know anyone in the entire state," Nancy pointed out. "You don't even ski. Tell me again: Why are you moving to Bend?"

Not entirely certain myself, I muttered something about the great Eddie Bauer outlet store, the cheap car registration, and, of course, my hair.

"So basically," Nancy said, "you're moving to Bend for beauty reasons?"

I had no idea what lay ahead for me in Bend—whether I'd make friends, whether I'd find happiness and true love. But yes, I was content, for the moment, knowing that my hair would look marvelous.

Day 1400
B.C.E.

Day 1
C.E.

Day 1000
C.E.

6

Home Sweet Home

$\mathscr{B}$ack in college I took an anthropology class that was widely known as a "gut," university-speak for a course so easy that your average laboratory rat could ace it. Given the reputation of this class and the fact that it met at 9 A.M., when I was typically sound asleep, I rarely showed up and almost never did the homework, assuming that I'd earn a respectable grade simply for having enrolled. As it happened, I failed the midterm and was awarded a zero for class participation, and by the time the final exam came around, my situation was dire: If I was going to pass this class, I had to—in one night—memorize the entirety of human evolution. Sadly, despite a twenty-hour, caffeine- and taco-fueled cram session, I didn't know *Australopithecus afarensis* from *Australopithecus africanus* and promptly flunked.

As I headed up to Bend in my Trooper, wondering what lay ahead and reflecting on all that had happened, it dawned on me that for years I had approached my life the same way I'd faced Anthro 101: I'd been coasting. I'd neglected to really apply myself, taking it on faith that if I just kept doing the minimum—taking whatever writing assignments came my way, flirting with whatever reasonable prospect happened by, being nice enough to let Grandma Ruth occasionally beat me at Scrabble—eventually I'd stumble upon the great guy, the fulfilling career, the satisfying life that I had always aspired to.

But what did I have to show for this slacker strategy? A string of second-rate ex-boyfriends, a bad *Law & Order* habit, and an income earned from rewriting "10 Minutes to Your Best Body" a hundred different ways. Even grading on a curve and awarding extra credit for my regular exercise routine, I was on the verge of flunking myself.

However, there was still plenty of time to turn things around. What lay before me now was the perfect opportunity to make dramatic changes. The coasting was over. From this point on I would operate on a single overriding principle: Life is what you make happen. Or, as Grandpa Julius likes to say, "You've got to write your own goddamn ticket, because it sure as hell isn't going to fall out of the sky."

Lollapasuza was just the start. Now I had to ramp up my efforts.

I arrived in Bend on a high, intoxicated by the crisp October air, my sense of resolve, and the brand-newness of the steel-blue house I had leased. Finished the week I moved in, it bore a vague resemblance to a barn, complete with a red door, and it featured a pine staircase made from a tree in the front yard that had been felled by lightning. I marveled that my two-story, three-bedroom home—just a mile from Bend's splendid downtown park and minutes from hiking, biking, and ski trails—cost me four hundred dollars a month less than the crummy apartment I'd been renting in Berkeley. I thought I was some kind of genius.

My first order of business was to create an atmosphere in my home that was just like Bend (and, of course, the New Me): cheerful, quirky, energetic. This would be a radical departure from my previous decor themes, which could charitably be described as "early nineties garage sale" and, in later years, "early nineties garage sale with Crate and Barrel nightstands." For years I'd lived in a series of almost interchangeable apartments furnished with hand-me-downs, including four ratty upholstered chairs, a stack of beige vinyl placemats, and the world's least-comfortable couch—a wicker number donated by my grandparents. (Grandpa Julius' rear end had become so bony—or, as he liked to say, "I've got a goddamn case of ass*itis*"—that he could no longer sit on it.) I'd never bothered to sink much money into furniture because I feared that whatever I bought wouldn't be right when I finally moved up from an apartment. But that day had finally come, and I was ready to dip into my savings.

Certain I'd live in Bend for years, if not forever, I vowed to start over with furnishings deliberately chosen to reflect my new life. The only stumbling block was that I had zero design sense. Left to my own devices, I worried my new home would become an exact replica of a Pottery Barn window display. But I knew whom to turn to for help: my sister.

Jen and I are just two years apart, but that's the only short distance between us. Growing up, we always seemed to maintain two separate orbits, even more so in high school. I spent my teens holed up in my bedroom pretending to do homework while compulsively watching *M*A*S*H* reruns and any TV show starring Lee Majors. In a stroke of good fortune for me, my parents had placed the family's only television in my bedroom. They were opposed to the concept of TV, not because they considered it insipid or destructive, but because of the damage they felt a TV set would inflict on the aesthetics of a room. They'd just as soon place a lawn mower in the living room as they would a twenty-five-inch Sony.

I have no clue how my sister spent her time while I survived six years of single-sex education by fantasizing about *The Six Million Dollar Man.* But I do know that she attended a coed, arts-oriented high school where the students produced a lot of plays, smoked a lot of drugs, and called the principal "Jim." After I went off to college, Jen and I never lived in the same city and talked infrequently. Yet over the years, we spent enough time together at family events to discover that we did have common ground, most notably on matters involving our well-meaning parents and our high-maintenance grandparents. We also grew to appreciate our respective abilities.

One of Jen's most obvious assets, in addition to the impeccable sense of style she inherited from our father, was her creativity. Her college thesis, titled "The Party as Performance," doubled as a formal cocktail affair. Guests were required to follow strict rules, conversing in certain areas only about designated topics, such as smoking or love or pets. I was certain that Jen's ingenuity and keen eye could do wonders for my new house in Bend.

So a few weeks after I moved in, I booked a flight for my sister, who was now pursuing her master's degree in New Genre, a field of study that, from what I could tell, involved wearing a lot of black. Jen darted out of Bend's tiny airport tugging at her red and yellow flannel shirt.

"I borrowed it!" she said breathlessly. "I just knew this was the kind of place where you wear plaid!"

From the moment she arrived, Jen and I worked at warp speed. She did a split-second assessment of my pine-trimmed house ("Okay, I get it," she said), then grabbed my car keys and commandeered my Trooper, whizzing past Bend's "25 mph" signs as I directed her to Central Oregon's numerous antique shops. I marveled at Jen's gifts. Walking into a shop, I'd be overwhelmed by the clutter of chairs and cabinets and mirrors and rugs and candlesticks, wondering if I could sort through it all before the store closed. But Jen would take one glance, make a beeline to the wonderful end table made from old post-office boxes, and announce, "I'll wait outside while you pay for it."

In just two days Jen and I amassed, for a remarkably small sum, a houseful of furniture and accessories—weathered pine chairs, handmade quilts, lamps made of wagon-wheel hubs, photos of local rivers. The final touch was a green metal *S*, not unlike Mary Tyler Moore's big *M*, which I nailed to my bedroom wall. In barely an instant, my new home now looked as if I'd lived there for years.

A few weeks after Jen left, my parents made their own pilgrimage to Bend, and I was excited to show them how my new life was taking shape. Like Jen, they emerged from the airport terminal wearing plaid, although they didn't brag so effusively about it.

My mother was carrying what appeared to be a large clear plastic case, and as she drew near, I made out what was inside: a folded queen-sized mattress pad. The woman had traveled thirteen hundred miles to bring me polyester bedding.

"I didn't know if they'd have these in Bend!" she said, holding up the extra-thick pad.

"Yes, Mom, they have running water, too!" I reassured her, adding that they also had low-fat cream cheese, which she had already inquired about on the phone.

During their weekend visit, I didn't bother to show my parents Bend's waterfalls, lakes, and desert trails because I knew, in true Schlosberg form, they wouldn't be interested. What my parents did want to see was my guest closet, where my father was alarmed to find I had no wooden hangers. (He considers plastic hangers to be an offense on the order of fake flowers.) My mother was distressed that I did not have designated guest towels in the bathroom.

"If all your towels are the same color," Mom asked, "how will your guests know which ones are yours and which are theirs?"

It was, I admitted, an issue I had not considered. I suggested we rectify my domestic oversights with a central Oregon cultural event: a trip to Wal-Mart. My parents looked stricken. As I expected, I was pushing them into uncharted territory.

"But they're so *big*," Mom said, aghast, as Dad nodded.

Still, I convinced them Wal-Mart would have the best selection of hangers and towels, so they reluctantly agreed to go. Once inside the store, I was able to pinpoint the source of their insecurity: They were surrounded by products they had no clue how to use. Belt sanders, Buck knives, Coleman stoves—these were not popular items among fine-art dealers in L.A.

We managed to purchase the hangers and towels without incident, and Mom was even impressed by the store's toaster display. Outside, my parents posed for a photograph in front of the Wal-Mart sign, beaming as if they had arrived by seaplane to an outer island of Borneo.

Back at my house, my mother organized the guest towels while my father developed a fixation with my gas heater, a faux wood-burning stove. To keep the flames rising from the imitation logs, Dad steadily cranked up the thermostat. At no point did he seem bothered that it was ninety-two degrees in my living room.

"It's just so cozy!" he said, marveling at the flames.

Over the course of their visit, my parents were enchanted by Bend's breakfast cafes, by the Jewish community's potluck dinner, by the downtown boutiques that sold flannel pajamas with pine tree prints. By the time they left Bend, they seemed to think I was living in a Disney movie with friendly bears.

I rated their visit a success. None of the Alec-related tensions had surfaced. To my great relief, my parents never even mentioned his name—not surprising, given that my family finds its comfort zone in tasks, not "issues." I was thrilled that they'd accepted my new environment, and I was more certain than ever that I'd made a wise choice.

Day 1400
B.C.E.

Day 1
C.E.

Day 1000
C.E.

7

Sex and the Small Town

*W*ithin weeks after moving to Bend, my life outside my new home had been transformed as completely as the interior. Back in Berkeley, I had rarely gotten out of my pajamas until the late afternoon, when I'd change into my workout clothes, and it wasn't uncommon for me to conduct phone interviews dripping wet and wearing a towel turban. (My hard-to-reach sources had the infuriating habit of calling right when I was getting out of the shower.) But now I was waking up early, getting dressed, and walking down the street to A Cup of Magic, a cozy coffee- and teahouse, where I'd nestle into a futon and sip a ginger peach smoothie while reading *USA Today*. Then I'd stroll home, past the snowboard shops and juice cafes, and settle into work. I was still writing articles about cellulite and exfoliants, but now I cranked them out at a faster pace to leave more time to enjoy my new surroundings.

Of course, there were some adjustments to small-town life. Not long after my move, I had a genuine cause for alarm: the apparent deterioration of my eyesight. After I found myself struggling to read street signs at night, I paid a visit to an ophthalmologist. But a battery of tests showed that my eyes were fine.

"So why can't I see?" I asked the doc.

"Because it's *dark* here," he said.

I was embarrassed that I hadn't noticed: except for downtown, Bend did not have streetlights. It would have taken Lee Majors' bionic eye to spot the turnoff to my street at fifty yards.

But I managed to adapt, and within a few weeks, I felt I was making progress in my effort to become a fully functional citizen of Bend. My strategy was to cover every angle, aiming for maximum exposure. I joined an organization for the self-employed—graphic designers, carpenters, and the like—enrolled in a volunteer literacy program, and started teaching an adult journalism course at the community college.

In anticipation of the first snowfall, I signed up for a cross-country ski class, hoping that it might include some new folks in town who were also novices. Besides, living in Bend without proficiency in at least one winter sport would be like living in Maui without knowing how to swim. Downhill skiing was out. As a kid, I'd never gotten past the snowplow stage, and I would only be disgraced by those Suzy Chapstick girls who probably came slaloming out of their mother's wombs. Cross-country skiing, which requires less coordination and more endurance, seemed a better fit.

I rounded out my activity schedule with events organized by Bend's Jewish community, most of whom were refugees from L.A. Yom Kippur services took place shortly after I moved to Bend, and I was heartened to find the con-

gregants as welcoming as they'd been during my Lollapasuza visit. One couple even invited me, on the spot, to
dinner after services. I left their home with such a warm
feeling that the next week I signed up for the Jewish community's weekly Hebrew class.

Of course, it was no coincidence that everything I was
doing in Bend had the potential of putting me in the prox-
imity of single guys. Well, everything except Hebrew. The
only male in the class was our teacher, Steve, who was in
his fifties and married.

Feeling inspired and confident and sporting frizz-free
curls, I even went so far as to split my workout time
between two different gyms. One had newer equipment but
a dismal layout for scoping, with the cardio machines fac-
ing the parking lot. The other club had some creaky
machinery but a much better floor plan, so I could survey
all the action from my perch on the StairMaster.

I suppose some people may view my swirl of activities as
edging toward the dismal side of over-thirty single woman-
hood known as "desperate." But I strongly disagree. Desperate
is when you abandon all hope of finding the guy you're looking for and settle instead for the guy you can tolerate, and I
was nowhere near that point. I was simply determined not to
miss any opportunities, and at least all of my activities were
things I was interested in doing. When you're thirty years old
and new in town, you recognize that Prince Charming isn't
likely to come knocking on your door, especially considering
the only people who ever do knock on your door are your
paperboy and your FedEx lady. (Just my luck. I couldn't even
rate a FedEx guy.)

It was only natural that I would step up my efforts in
response to a faintly ticking clock and that I would, on

occasion, do that mathematical calculation known to single women in their thirties as the Best-Case Scenario. You know, the one that goes like this: "Okay, even if I meet Mr. Right *today*, like, this afternoon, then the soonest I could get married would be a year and a half, including one year to fall in love, get in a huge fight, almost break up, make up with incredible sex, meet our respective families, then recover from meeting our respective families—plus six months for the engagement, so that the marriage is viewed by friends and relatives as the act of love it truly is rather than a spur-of-the-moment decision that's sure to turn into a fiasco. Then I have to add another year, preferably two— allowing for a general adjustment to being married, plus a last-hurrah trip to Tahiti—before I start trying to get pregnant. Factoring in a year, just in case, for fertility counseling, I'm talking five and a half years before I own my first Diaper Genie. That is—best-case scenario—five and a half years from *this exact moment*."

Of course, I wasn't entertaining these thoughts on a regular basis. In truth, I felt I had enough breathing room to fit in a few flings and a rebound relationship before finding a guy who amounted to husband material.

My new schedule of activities didn't produce any immediate flirtations, but I did meet several women who offered to set me up with eligible guys. Now, normally, I would have declined the offers, because the few blind dates I'd been on back home had been such debacles. Among the worst: a setup with a mohel—yes, a man who performs ritual circumcisions on Jewish male infants—who had quit his obstetrics practice because, he said, "Women were having babies at all hours of the night. Now, it's like, snip-snip, five-hundred bucks, and I'm outta there."

But since I'd gone into Bend blind, it only seemed appropriate to meet men that way, too. In the spirit of hopefulnesss, I now agreed to all of the setups presented to me.

One of my first dates, a photographer, was witty and handsome—if you ignored the waist-length braid that fell down his back, which I tried very hard to do. But he canceled our second date because he had to call the sheriff. Apparently, his ex-wife was violating the restraining order. I never got a raincheck and decided it was just as well.

Twice I went to dinner with a cute blond insurance broker, but eventually conversation degenerated into a discussion of our respective disability policies. Undaunted, I shared a pizza with a boyishly handsome engineer, but he seemed too obsessed with cross-country skiing. He tracked how many days he skied each year and how many consecutive months he'd skied (seventy-eight and counting), and once he used the term "we"—as in "we skied in the backcountry yesterday"—in reference to himself and his *skis*.

I had my first flicker of hope with a software developer who was sharp and easy to talk to and also happened to be Jewish. He was alarmingly thin—I could easily have benchpressed him—and had wavy shoulder-length hair that was none too flattering. Still, as much as I disliked the hair, I feared the outcome if he cut it, since it was the only part of him that had any volume. Initially I wasn't attracted to the guy, whom I referred to as the LHJ, the Long-Haired Jew, to distinguish him, in reports to my friends, from the LHP, the Long-Haired Photographer, but I decided to give him a chance. After all, the instant attraction I'd had with Alec had gotten me nowhere.

On about our fourth date, the LHJ and I went to Lava Lanes for "cosmic bowling," one of Bend's prime Saturday-night attractions, featuring glow-in-the-dark pins. I'm not sure why—probably because the lights were dimmed and I'd already suffered several months without sex—but that night the LHJ's butt looked sort of appealing. When he invited me to his place afterward, I confessed that I found him attractive. He smiled, took my hand, and escorted me to his bedroom. We'd removed all of our clothes and were busy groping each other under the covers when he abruptly stopped.

"You know," he announced, "I'm tired of taking test drives that end up lasting three years."

I wasn't sure I understood, but he quickly drew a clear picture. "I want to save myself. The next car I drive will be for keeps," he said, clearly suggesting I was not the model he was looking for.

I was utterly speechless, no doubt because I was having such difficulty deciding which pissed me off more: being compared to an automobile or being rejected while lying in his bed naked. He said I could still stay over, but he wasn't going to have sex with me. If it hadn't been 3 A.M. and the dead of winter, I would have left that second. But I hadn't fully adapted to Bend's subfreezing overnight temperatures, and I couldn't muster the energy to put back on my four layers of clothes, then go sit in the car for ten minutes as I waited for it to warm up. So, silently fuming, I took the path of least resistance, turned over, and forced myself to go to sleep. The date ended awkwardly in the morning, with the LHJ and I agreeing to be the "friends" we would never be.

Although the LHJ was a jerk, I reminded myself that he was, in fact, the first jerky guy I'd encountered in Bend. But even as I was congratulating myself for getting back into circulation, I realized an unexpected complication was creeping into the picture. Being around the LHJ, with his spindly arms and irritating vehicle analogies, only reminded me of what I'd left behind in Berkeley. In truth, I couldn't help but compare all of my dates to Alec. He may have had his blockhead tendencies, but at least he didn't have a psycho ex-wife or believe his skis were his friends or wear his hair like Shaggy from *Scooby-Doo*.

I'd assumed that by leaving the past behind and throwing all my energy into making over my life, I could painlessly adjust to the breakup. But instead, all I'd done was postpone the inevitable. A couple months after the move, it became clear that I was in the clutches of Ex-Boyfriend Withdrawal Syndrome.

The major symptom, of course, is that maddening, relentless impulse to pick up the phone and call him. Like a two-pack-a-day smoker trying to kick the habit, you're in a constant state of temptation and rationalization: *What's so wrong with just wanting to say hi? Maybe he's wondering how I'm doing. Maybe he wants to call but doesn't have the nerve. Or wait—maybe I left something important at his house!*

Every time I'd find my hand dangerously hovering over the phone, I'd remind myself how badly things had ended with Alec. Then, like an AA member turning to my sponsor instead of the bottle, I'd call one of my cabinet members for another reminder. All had agreed to be on standby duty.

A couple months into my Bend residency I came up with my weirdest strategy for stopping myself from calling Alec: I called the Bend Police Department instead. On the pretext of wanting to better acquaint myself with my new community, I scheduled a ride-along on Saturday night. Perhaps a night with any cop, I thought, would help cure me of my cop. Or better yet, maybe I'd find a hunky guy on the force who was looking for some off-duty action.

My spirits rose when I was assigned to a muscular, twenty-seven-year-old officer with a crew cut, but ten minutes into the patrol shift, he was happily chatting about his wife, his four-year-old, and "the new baby." I was forced to spend the next five hours feigning interest in the workings of the Bend PD, dredging up the cop lingo I'd picked up from Alec and asking questions like, "So, what's your department's policy on vehicle pursuits?" and "Do your lieutenants get out on the street much?" Of course, all I really wanted to know was, "Do you have any single officers who want to get laid?"

The shift was painfully short on action. We stopped two men for bicycling at night without a headlight and took a report of a stolen car stereo. I wished that I'd stayed home and watched *Cops*.

My lowest moment was on New Year's Eve, a holiday not known for perking up single, dateless women in isolated towns who have made no plans for the evening. In a full-fledged funk, I ordered take-out from a burger joint, picked up an Oreo Blizzard at Dairy Queen, then went home and watched *Short Cuts*, a three-and-a-half-hour Robert Altman film about infidelity, murder, rape, alcoholism, wife beating, fear, boredom, loneliness, and misery.

I woke up on New Year's Day feeling blue and antsy, so I tossed an overnight bag and my road atlas in the Trooper and headed southeast across the desert on a desolate two-lane highway, with no particular destination in mind. Glancing at the map, I noticed I was about four hundred miles away from Winnemucca, Nevada, a remote mining and gambling town where I'd once spent the night on a road trip with Alec.

That was it—the perfect destination! True, Winnemucca was nothing more than a dreary dot on the map with a handful of cheap motels. But there was something comfortable and familiar about going back to a place where Alec and I had had good times, sort of like visiting an old house that used to be yours. With a new sense of purpose, I stepped harder on the gas. Eight hours later—having passed a total of six cars and one gas station and realizing if I spun out on the icy road, I might not be found for days—I came to the edge of town. Before me stood a billboard that announced, in giant black letters, "Winnemucca: Where Life Begins."

For me, life in Winnemucca began as the only customer at a twenty-four-hour diner. I was served a greasy grilled-cheese sandwich and a bed of wilted iceberg lettuce by a rotation of plump, husky-voiced waitresses who never put down their cigarettes. I then checked into the Super 8—mustering the willpower to avoid the Pyrenees Motel, where Alec and I had stayed—and crashed hard. The next morning I worked out at Winnemucca's only gym and played some nickel slots at a nearly deserted casino. I then drove back across the desert at ninety miles an hour, arriving in Bend thirty-one hours after I'd left, just in time for *Homicide*.

When I called Nancy to tell her about my trip, she was incredulous. "Wait," she said, "you're telling me you just drove nine hundred miles to use a StairMaster?"

"Well, the Super 8 did have country videos on cable," I offered, but Nancy cut me off.

"I still don't know where Bend is," she said, "but please get the fuck out of there."

"What are you talking about?" I protested. "I just got here."

I stridently rose to Bend's defense. If anything, the bleakness of Winnemucca had given me a new perspective about my home, and I now had a greater appreciation for all its pleasing qualities—its pine forests, calm lakes, soymilk smoothies, chiseled (if long-haired) outdoorsmen. I argued to Nancy that I'd met lots of friendly people and had discovered the joy of romping through the mountains on snowshoes. A couple from L.A. had even opened Bend's first Jewish deli, serving real bagels, not the Wonder-Bread-in-a-circle variety sold at Safeway.

Besides, my hair was looking superb: The crisp winter air left my curls in perfect ringlets, and I'd found Robert, a talented hairdresser who charged just twenty-four dollars for a cut and blowdry.

Nancy was unmoved. "So, like, who are you planning to have sex with, your Hebrew teacher?"

I had to concede that my prospects, so far, were not fabulous.

Over the next several weeks, I thought about Alec more than usual. Then one night in mid-February, I came up with what I concluded was my first ironclad credible reason to dial his number: I had set a new personal record on the bench press! After all the time we'd spent lifting weights together, surely Alec would want to know about this new milestone in my life. So certain that I'd waited for the right moment, I skipped over my friends on standby and paged Alec. He called right back and offered that he'd been thinking about me.

"Really?" I said, already glad that I'd called.

"Yeah, I was thinking about how great it was that I didn't have to buy anyone a Valentine's Day card this year. So, have you seen the new Brooks and Dunn video?"

From his tone, I knew he meant it as a joke, but still I was crushed. My ex-boyfriend was happy, and all I had going for me were two more plates on the bench press.

We talked for fifteen minutes. I asked Alec about his mother and his truck and his friend Bruce, who'd transferred from patrol to traffic. He was friendly, but didn't say much more besides answering my questions.

So I'd done it. First contact. And it probably wasn't that much different than if I'd just talked to a space alien. Once again, the eternal question remained unanswered: How can guys shut off their emotions like a garden spigot, and why do women always expect them not to?

I guess you could argue that women are predisposed to expending their emotions at the drop of a hat (or the airing of a Kodak commercial), while men seem to have the innate ability to treat their emotions like a bad business investment. So is it any wonder women always expect a different outcome? Silly romantics that we are, we run through just as many emotions leaving a relationship as we do entering it. (And, of course, that's why women are almost always the "first callers"—that is, unless the guy happened to leave his bicycle wrench lying on the floor of your closet and now wants it back.) Meanwhile, in the face of a breakup, men employ their insufferable practicality. If they see the relationship is about to go belly-up, the only sensible thing to do is cut their losses and declare emotional bankruptcy.

Why the difference? Who knows? It's like gravity. It's there. It's irrefutable. It holds sway over our lives, yet nobody has ever figured out why.

After I hung up with Alec, I could have run to the nearest mirror and said, "I told you so," but there really was little to regret about making the phone call. It simply reinforced why I was no longer with Alec, as if I needed reinforcement (and I guess I did). But even more important, it proved to be the Cure. Any compulsion to call him vanished from that day on.

I suppose that meant I'd made it over one more hurdle, but there was no exhilaration. In fact, after five months in Bend, I was growing weary—of putting myself out there, of introducing myself to new people, of memorizing Hebrew vocabulary. I wanted to keep going, but I needed to find a way to recharge.

Day 1400
B.C.E.

Day 1
C.E.

Day 1000
C.E.

8

A Walk on the Wild Side

I was at Wal-Mart buying a snow shovel when the solution struck: Nairobi!

Nairobi was where my college friend Julie had been based for three years, engaged in public-health research that she claimed was too complicated to explain. She regularly traveled to places such as Uganda and Malawi and Burkina Faso, but all she ever talked about in her e-mails was how painful it was to use the construction paper masquerading as toilet tissue.

For the longest time, she'd been pestering me to visit her in Kenya, but between my preoccupations with Alec, then Bend, I'd never seriously considered it. Now, though, I had to wonder: If you feel like you're getting nowhere, isn't that the time to go somewhere else?

Winnemucca had been a head-clearing diversion, but it hadn't been nearly far enough or long enough. What I needed was a complete break from the humdrum, a change of scenery where I didn't know what would be around the next corner. I wanted to feel that sense of possibility again. And anyway, on even the best vacations you eventually start to miss your own bed. Maybe a trip to a faraway place would make Bend feel more like home.

So I drove back from Wal-Mart and booked a flight—actually, about six flights, Bend not being the gateway to East Africa. A month after that, I set off from Bend, and forty-six hours later arrived at Julie's three-bedroom apartment in the heart of Nairobi. Feeling like a flattened sofa bolster that needed to be fluffed back to its proper shape, I was overcome with relief—and not simply because I could sleep as long as I wanted in an actual bed. It was just nice to be around someone I had history with. In Bend, I was having to rehash my life story on a daily basis. But Julie had known me forever, since the days when we both had feathered hair. I didn't have to explain my crush on Sam Waterston or my obsession with veal parmesan (our favorite dorm entrée), or my belief that half-birthdays should be celebrated. Julie pulled out the Scrabble, popped in a tape of our favorite movie, *This Is Spinal Tap,* and we picked up where we'd last left off, in her Manhattan apartment five years earlier. Already I could hear Nancy's reaction: "Wait, you're telling me you flew halfway around the world to play a board game and watch videos?"

Julie and I hung out for a couple of days, but then I was on my own, since she didn't happen to have three spare weeks to show me around Kenya. (However, she did let me tag along on one of her work expeditions, which finally resolved the matter of what she was doing to help humanity: sitting around a table with a bunch of people arguing about the wording of demographic surveys.) At the time of my visit, tourism in Kenya was at an all-time low due to a flurry of stabbings, shootings, university riots, and deaths from cholera, malaria, and Rift Valley fever. But Julie said this was great news for me: She'd gotten me a bargain rate at a luxury lodge in one of Kenya's premier game parks, Amboseli, known for its herds of wild elephants and wildebeest and its view of Mount Kilimanjaro. I figured I couldn't get much more of a change of scenery than that.

I was the only passenger on the six-seater plane that flew me to the bush. A Land Rover delivered me to the lodge, a cluster of two dozen canvas-roofed huts nestled in a grove of acacia trees. About fifteen valets in crisp burgundy uniforms were there to welcome me and vie to carry my day pack. A small entourage led me to my luxury tent, which featured a king-sized bed, modern toilet facilities (complete with soft, two-ply tissue), and a private veranda where a small pot of tea was waiting for me. Although I did enjoy the royal treatment, I couldn't help but feel I was on a honeymoon without benefit of a husband.

The lodge was eerily quiet—think *The Shining* meets *Out of Africa*—but it was not until the first night, in the elegant open-air dining area, that I discovered just how empty the place really was: Besides me, there was only one guest. But what luck! He was tall and broad-shouldered with thick, dark hair and a vague resemblance to Pierce Brosnan.

Maybe it was because of our exotic surroundings, but suddenly I saw a whole new future stretched before me, and it was right out of a steamy Hollywood screenplay. A seemingly innocent invitation for an after-dinner drink on the veranda, a provocative exchange of dialogue under the moonlit sky. The charming stranger takes my hand, and I follow him into the bedroom, where we rip each other's clothes off and leap into bed for a long night of hot, sweaty sex. The next morning, we toast the wonders of Africa, the serendipity that brought us together, and the unexpected rewards of traveling solo while agreeing, of course, that this is just a tawdry vacation affair. How great it was, I thought, to have a life with so much possibility!

But first I had to meet this mystery man, a task that presented a bit of a challenge since we were seated four tables apart. As a brigade of bored waiters and busboys watched the first scenes of our drama unfold, my dinner companion and I spent several minutes glancing over at each other, nodding, then quickly averting our eyes to our respective plates. Finally, after the salad course, I walked over to his table, introduced myself, and asked if I could join him. He said he would be delighted.

Within seconds, my new companion, George, and I made a remarkable discovery. We were both from Oregon! Forget the tawdry-movie genre. This was right out of a Tom Hanks–Meg Ryan romantic comedy. Living a mere thirty-five minutes apart by plane but having to travel twelve thousand miles to the African bush to meet and fall in love! I could see us now—sitting at home on the deck of our pine-trimmed cottage in Oregon, toasting the wonders of Africa, the strange twist of fate that brought us together, and our first year of wedded bliss.

I was jolted out of fantasyland a few minutes later, when I realized that George, a history professor from Portland, was in fact a pompous ass. Without any prompting, he informed me that he had won a teacher-of-the-year award twice, had written twelve books, and was in the thirty-nine-percent tax bracket.

I spent three interminable days with George, sharing not only meals but also a Land Rover on our game drives.

It didn't take long for me to add "boring" to "pompous ass." Not that the elephants weren't impressive, but it was a little hard to enjoy the primal beauty of Africa while sitting next to a guy who brought along a camera store's worth of equipment and kept saying things like, "To take the edge off the hard highlights, you need to dial in minus compensation and shoot with an F4 AFS on a Gitzo carbon fiber 1548."

By the end of my stay at Amboseli, I was ready to hurl myself in front of a charging herd of wildebeest.

At this point, I was beginning to grasp some of the drawbacks of traveling alone, such as the potential of being held hostage with an exasperating stranger. (George wasn't the only accidental traveling companion who drove me bonkers. On a train ride to Kenya's coast, I shared a bunk bed with a nine-year-old girl who sang the same Coke jingle, almost nonstop, for fourteen hours.) Plus traveling solo means you don't have anyone to share your misadventures with. For me, that practically took all the fun out of being stalked for hours by a carved-rhino salesman and almost getting killed in a taxi with no inside door handles, a smashed windshield, and a bumper sticker that said "May God bless my hands so that I may drive safely."

By the time my trip ended, I was more than ready to return to cozy Bend. I knew I was headed in the right direction when, on the final leg of my journey home, a late-night flight from Portland, it dawned on me that I had not arranged for transportation from the airport. As we were landing, I instinctively blurted out, "Hey, would anyone mind giving me a ride to the Westside?" In Kenya—or in L.A., for that matter—I might as well have been asking, "Hey, does anybody want to abduct me, sexually assault me, and leave me for dead in a drainage ditch?" But in Bend, you could actually accept a ride from a stranger without fear. Right away I had an offer from a long-haired teenage snowboarder. "No problem," he said. "I'm heading to the Eastside, but I'll drop you off." What a swell place!

When I opened my front door that night, I felt the surge I'd been hoping for. It was great to be back. Winnemucca had given me a taste of the drab, and Kenya had given me a taste of the exotic—and both extremes had made Bend seem more appealing than ever. Looking at the town with fresh eyes, I remembered why I'd fallen in love with it in the first place. Yeah, I was a little lonely, but surely it was better to be lonely in your own home. Over the next several days, I settled back into my routine, more determined than ever to make Bend work for me.

Day 1400
B.C.E.

Day 1
C.E.

Day 1000
C.E.

9

Lost in Sex Camp

It's remarkable what a six-month dry spell will do to your outlook. At any other time in my life, if someone had uttered the words "Club Med," I'd have rolled my eyes and scoffed, "Why would I want to spend seven days at a manufacturing plant for fake romance?" But that's not how I responded a few weeks after returning from Kenya, when an editor at a women's fitness magazine asked me to write about an adults-only Club Med. I surprised myself when I jumped at the chance. Club Med would be a sure thing, like fishing in a stocked pond!

The resort, Turkoise, was located on the Turks and Caicos Islands, just west of the Caribbean, and the company's Web site described the place as one of Club Med's "most social" villages. Photos showed bronzed and beautiful people swimming, sailing, and strolling hand in hand under the swaying palm trees. "The idea here is simple: Enjoy yourself," the site said. "There are no strangers here—at least not for long." It sounded like I was getting a free trip to the Disney World of coupling up.

I'd made a quick and contented reentry into my Bend activities upon my return from Kenya, but I didn't see how I could get too detoured with such a lark. To get into the spirit, I purchased a couple tropical ensembles at a Bend store called At the Beach. (I'd often wondered who, in a fleece-obsessed ski town, was spending money there. Now I knew.) Then I jetted off for New York City, where I picked up a charter flight to Providenciales, the main Turks and Caicos island.

Surveying my fellow passengers—the cliques of Long Island party girls, high-fiving former frat boys, sheepish divorced dads, and executive types waiting to bust loose— I sensed I was about to embark on a grown-up version of the "American history" teen tour I took one summer in high school (in reality, a tour of the nation's fast-food franchises with the occasional historical monument thrown in). I remember boarding the bus that first day, brimming with anticipation as I surveyed my fellow tenth-graders. I marveled at the cute girls in miniskirts—the girls clearly destined to become popular on the trip—and wondered if I, wearing Bermuda shorts, might have a chance of joining them in pursuit of the cute, destined-to-be-popular boys on the bus. But six weeks later, the only success I'd had was in fending off the overtures of Howard, a gangly baseball card fanatic who wore tube socks and had one of those premustaches. As the jet lifted off the runway at Kennedy Airport, I hoped I would do better at Club Med.

Within moments of stepping off the plane and into the Caribbean humidity, my hair expanded to the size of a circus balloon. Meanwhile, the damp air was having the opposite effect on my dress, which was now clinging to my thighs. Once aboard the bus on the way to Club Med, I scanned the surroundings, looking for my tropical paradise, but I was shocked to find there wasn't a palm tree in sight. Providenciales, known by the locals as "Provo," was a sandy, scrub-covered wasteland dotted with banks, insurance companies, and convenience stores—the kind of place that screamed, "Do your offshore money laundering here!" I was beginning to wonder if we'd landed on the wrong island until we drove through the gates of the Club Med compound. Instantly, the scenery morphed into such an explosion of palm trees and bougainvillea that I felt like I'd been escorted into a B movie shot in Technicolor.

Filing off the bus, we were run through a gantlet of cheering Club Med employees who did what I could only describe as the visual equivalent of squeezing the produce. The other guests seemed to enjoy the attention, but with my frizzed-out hair and stick-on dress, I couldn't run fast enough.

Our orders were to take our luggage to our rooms and report back immediately for orientation. I was directed to a complex of what looked like community-college dorms and found my room on the second floor. It had no TV or telephone, but to me all that mattered was the air conditioner in the window, which I promptly plastered myself against. Once I'd cooled down enough to peel the fabric from my thighs, I wandered over to the orientation at the open-air theater.

On the walk over, I could see the resort had been planned for optimum fun in the sun for the six hundred or so guests—with its two pools, beach volleyball pits, basketball and tennis courts. Signs near the beach directed you to the scuba shack and waterskiing dock. Practically every venue was bustling with activity, and I wondered if as much activity was going on between couples back in the rooms.

Surely the liveliest spot in the place was the orientation, a spectacle led by the village chief, a fortyish, eternally tanned Spaniard named Lulu whose long brown hair offered better coverage than her blue satin bikini. Shuffling like a prizefighter, Lulu introduced her staff—the chief of water sports, the chief of tennis, the chief of margaritas, and so on—and each was received by the audience with the kind of enthusiasm normally reserved for the Super Bowl's starting offense. She explained how to use the Club Med lingo: Staff members were GOs, short for *Gentils Organisateurs*, so named by Club Med's French management, or Gracious Organizers. Guests were GMs, or *Gentils Membres*.

Then Lulu made her announcements, punctuating them with Club Med's signature cheer—a high-pitched screeching noise that sounded like a Canada goose during mating season. Most of my travel companions already were well versed in the custom and happily screeched along with her. Try as I might, I found myself incapable of getting into the screeching spirit. In fact, the only thing the noise evoked in me was a single question: *Who are these people?*

Over the course of the week, I found out just about all I ever wanted to know about GMs. First of all, calling Club Med a "singles haven" is like calling the Sopranos a "family from New Jersey." The description simply doesn't do justice to all the complexities. Indeed, the Turkoise resort was its own erotically powered minisociety where complete strangers converged, hell-bent on finding mutual attraction. Little psychodramas played out every moment of every day—the advances and flirtations, the snap assessments (*Is he cute enough? Am I drunk enough?*), then it was either all systems go or the brush-off. Whether or not the outcome was sex (and from what I picked up in conversation, there did seem to be plenty of GMs back in their rooms getting it on), the two consenting parties tended to move on in search of more coming attractions.

But this wasn't a one-size-fits-all mating ritual. GMs naturally flocked to their own kind, which meant the resort was split squarely down the middle by age thirty, the Great Divide. On one side were the tanned and carefree twenty-somethings, effortlessly working the bar, the beach, and the pool. On the other side were the over-thirties, slathered in sunblock and looking as if they were trying a little too hard to have fun.

For the younger crowd, generous amounts of frozen margaritas seemed to be the only prerequisite to a good time. The older ones, though, apparently needed actual planned activities—windsurfing classes, snorkeling excursions, water polo. Afterward, they too convened around margaritas.

And then there was me—at age thirty, sitting atop the Great Divide. Looking one direction, I knew I had left behind those days when adulthood basically meant paying your own cable bill and marriage seemed as irrelevant as a pension plan. But looking the other way, I wondered, Was I about to become one of Them?

For a week, at least, the answer was yes. My magazine assignment virtually assured it, since I was required by my editor to do all the activities the over-thirties were flocking to. Now, only time would tell whether I would be, like on the teen tour, one of the cool people or a loser.

My baptism was immediate. The afternoon after orientation, during my first meal in the compound cafeteria, I plunged headfirst into the Club Med lifestyle. A hostess had put me at a table of over-thirties, and before I could even spear a garbanzo bean in my salad, the perky blonde to my right turned to me and said, "So, I told the tennis instructor there's, like, *no way* I'm sleeping with him. I mean, yeah, I'll fool around, but, like, if he thinks he's getting more, then, like, he's totally an idiot."

To which I could only think to reply, "I'm Suzanne. Have we met?"

The guy to my left, who looked like Barney Fife, only thinner and with a larger Adam's apple, explained that he and his roommate had developed a secret code system involving rubber bands on the doorknob, in case one of them happened to "catch some action."

Not quite sure how to respond to that conversation-starter, I mumbled something about looking forward to the snorkeling and tried to remind myself why I'd wanted to go on this trip in the first place. I was, after all, in the midst of lots of guys who were highly motivated to have a fling. All I had to do was find one who highly motivated me.

Early in the week, I experienced a distinct flicker of hope. I spent an afternoon lounging by the pool in twenty-something land, where I thought I'd lucked into a handsome financial analyst with a British accent. But after a few minutes of pleasant conversation, he squeezed my biceps and said, "I never did understand why a woman would lift weights," then got up and walked away. Considering that my arms did not exactly look like Xena, Warrior Princess', I wanted to yell back, "Hey, I never did understand why a man would want love handles!" But I decided against it.

Unfortunately, that was about as good as it got. After about forty-eight hours, I'd partaken of the whole resort experience enough to conclude that the men who came to

Club Med for a fling were not in the demographic of men I wanted to have flung.

Perhaps the most shining example of this was a tall, slender GM with dirty blond hair whom I encountered poolside. With no prompting, apropos of nothing, and to nobody in particular, he announced, "You know, I once posed nude in *Hustler*." He then dashed off to his room only to return with a copy of the magazine, which he proceeded to parade around to a group of us. I confess that, purely out of morbid curiosity, I took a glance myself. What I saw was shocking. Not the photo, but the date at the bottom of the page. This particular issue of *Hustler* was twelve years old.

I took a quick mental inventory of all the humiliating things I had done in my life and decided that none had come close to traveling with a twelve-year-old photo of myself naked.

Once I determined that all hope for sex was lost, my mood took a downturn, but I rebounded by reminding myself that, unlike the other GMs, I was getting paid to be there. For the sake of my assignment, I soldiered on with a full schedule of Club Med activities.

One morning I attended a stretching class taught by a grumpy Belgian woman who could have used a couple of assistants to help keep her breasts within the confines of her white, sequined leotard. "Okay," she instructed, "now we bounce," which she seemed to do without moving a muscle. (Never mind that, if she had read any one of the seventy-eight versions of "Firmer Abs, Thinner Thighs" I had written, she would have known that bouncing is now considered verboten.)

Later I went to water aerobics, where the instructor directed us to form a circle and massage the person in front of us. Reluctantly, I grazed my fingers on the stooped shoulders of the Arnold Horshack look-alike ahead of me. Then I glanced back and saw that my neck was being stroked by a flabby middle-aged Frenchman whose left-side comb-over was now plastered down the right side of his face. I slithered away and sprinted to my room for a shower and a nap.

At the snorkeling venue, a GO instructed the fifty of us in line to double up, and before I could even scout out my options, a knock-kneed woman named Shirley squealed, "So, we'll be partners, right?" Our group was then herded onto a boat and transported to a coral reef about a thousand yards offshore. After we squeezed into our masks and fins and jumped overboard, I quickly discovered there were more GMs in the water than fish. Fifteen minutes later, I gave up, climbed back in the boat, and spent the next half-hour relishing my time alone. I was enjoying a mininap on deck when I was startled awake by a familiar squeal. "We were supposed to stay *together*," snapped Shirley. "Those were the *rules*. That wasn't *safe*. It wasn't safe at *all*."

I couldn't believe how much I could hate someone I had known for less than two hours.

Although I fully admit the vast majority of GMs, young and old, seemed to think the resort was nirvana, I did occasionally bump into people who, like me, felt that a week at Motel 6 in Des Moines would have been preferable. One day at lunch I lent an ear to a chubby, despondent pathologist in his mid forties. He practically wept when I mentioned that my journalist status had scored me a single room. Most of the GMs had been randomly paired with roommates, and his had locked him out for three consecutive nights. "The only time he let me in," the doctor said, "was to help him find his Zoloft."

You know the movie *Groundhog Day,* where Bill Murray relives the same hellish day over and over and over again until he finally gets it right? That's exactly what Club Med eventually became to me—except I never got it right. Each day, the same activities were scheduled at the same place and the same time. At noon by the pool, the staff would line up and lead the GMs in a dance involving elaborate hand gestures and the words "sunshine," "moonlight," and "boogie." Every afternoon, the guy at the piano bar would sing the same songs in the same order. I swore that if I heard "Candle in the Wind" one more time the rest of my life, I would drown myself in a vat of frozen margaritas. The nightly entertainment was usually a musical/comedy act involving lip-synching and men in drag, with and without water balloons shoved down their tube tops.

By midweek, I'd gathered enough material for the upbeat story I was being paid to write and began hiding in the one place on the premises that was always empty: the gym. No one had traveled to the Caribbean to use the StairMaster.

It was near the end of my trip, one night at dinner, that I was reminded of one of Grandpa Julius' favorite sayings: "Nothing's so bad that it couldn't be worse." I was seated next to Sally, a weathered blond Provo resident who was visiting Club Med for the evening out of curiosity. My jaw dropped as she told her tragic tale. Married for twenty years and living in Manhattan, she had left her husband for an artist and on a whim had moved with him to Provo, sinking all her money into a house on the island that she'd found on the Internet. It wasn't until Sally and her new lover had settled in that she discovered he was a penniless alcoholic, that their tropical paradise was a scrub-covered refuge for drug smugglers, and that her dream house was worthless. Now she was stranded in Provo, unable to unload her property, desperate for customers at the beach-wear shop she'd opened, and in trouble with the local government for tax evasion.

Meeting Sally gave me a new tolerance for Club Med. If she could endure two years in Provo, surely I could handle three more days at the Turkoise compound.

But that was before I took the Sunset Singles' Cruise my editor insisted on. Last to arrive on the boat, I got stuck next to a chinless, slump-shouldered assistant tire-store manager from the Bronx whose toenails were so long they looked like guitar picks. I fled to the other side of the boat, where I ended up seated next to a woman on her fifth trip to Club Med Turkoise. She broke the ice by telling me she was "absolutely, completely sure" she had owned her two golden retrievers in a previous life.

By day five, I had discovered a coping strategy even better than the StairMaster: I was sleeping fourteen hours a day.

At dinner on the seventh and final night, I felt I had one last burst of friendliness in me, so I introduced myself to the sixtyish man sitting across the table. He had skin like beef jerky and dyed brown hair that was turning orange from the sun.

"So, where are you from?" I said, falling back on the typical Club Med opening line.

"Club Med," he said.

"No, I mean, where do you *live*?"

"Club Med."

He explained that he was "retired from pharmaceuticals" and for five years had been carting three suitcases from village to village, staying a month or two at a time, with no home base. He didn't mind that he had no access to newspapers, TV, or the outside world and did not consider his lifestyle a hindrance to building long-term relationships. Just recently at a village in Mexico, he said, he'd fallen for a Frenchwoman who had gladly quit her job in Paris to join him at Club Med. Alas, the relationship didn't work out. "After two weeks," he said wistfully, "we realized we weren't in love. Maybe it was the age difference." She was twenty-three. He sent her back to Paris and was searching for a replacement.

On the bus ride back to the airport, disappointment, particularly among the women, was palpable. Their experiences seemed to fall into two categories: Either they hadn't gotten laid, or their sex partners had discarded them like gum wrappers. That was when I realized I'd done the impossible. I'd spent the entire week at Turkoise without becoming either popular or a loser.

If Club Med did anything, it reminded me how good I had it in Bend. After Nairobi and Provo, I was done with wanderlust, and I was ready to settle back down to plain old lust.

Day 1400
B.C.E.

Day 1
C.E.

Day 1000
C.E.

10

Bent

$\mathcal{I}$ celebrated my thirty-first birthday with a cute, bright single guy, which would have been a wonderful turn of events if not for the fact that he was thirteen years old.

My birthday happened to fall on the day of his bar mitzvah, Bend's second ever. A few months earlier, I'd attended the community's first, a milestone event that had filled the Methodist-church basement. I didn't even know Bar Mitzvah Boy Number Two, but I worried that the novelty might have worn off and the folding chairs would be empty for his big day. In a gesture of goodwill, I decided to show up (a sacrifice made easier by the fact that I had nothing else to do). At the potluck dinner afterward, someone mentioned that it was my birthday, at which point the sixty-something membership chairwoman turned to me in horror and said, "And you're spending it with *us*?"

I returned home from the potluck to a birthday voice mail from my grandparents.

"I hope you get married while I'm still alive," Grandma Honey said.

"You know, thirty-one is older than thirty," Grandpa chimed in.

I lay down on my bed recalling my thirtieth birthday, which I had spent as Alec's girlfriend on the island of Pohnpei, near Guam. What was I now? A bar mitzvah groupie.

Birthdays have a way of turning the faint ticking into a loud bonging, at least for the day. And considering what was—and wasn't—happening in my life, I was hearing this one like Big Ben at high noon.

Life in Bend, I had to admit, wasn't exactly turning out as I had planned. Certainly, no one could have accused me of not trying. I'd joined, bowled, decorated, dated, skied, taught, memorized, cycled, StairMastered, and fleeced my way into the life of the town, but after almost a year's worth of effort, I still hadn't found anyone in Bend to share my new life with. I hadn't even come close.

I'd started arriving at this sobering realization a couple months before, when I got back from my week at Club Med. Waiting for me when I walked in the door were two insistent voice-mail messages from my friend Jillian.

"Call this guy Steve Meyer," she said on the first. "He's a writer and he's free Saturday night."

A few hours later: "I'm serious—you've got to call this guy."

Given Jillian's enthusiasm, I was so optimistic that I didn't even phone her back for my usual background check. Instead, I called Steve directly, and we agreed to meet for coffee the next day. He said he'd be wearing a brown leather jacket.

When I walked into Starbucks, I saw only one man wearing a brown leather jacket, a man whose hair—what was left of it—circled the base of his skull in one of those Alan Arkin fringes. Not that I mind men who are prematurely bald, except he wasn't one of them. I pegged him at fifty-five. We squinted at each other, and finally—incredulously—I said, "Are you . . . Steve?"

Both embarrassed, we stammered and made our way from the counter to a table, where I quickly learned two facts about Steve Meyer: (1) He had met Jillian just three days earlier, in Bend's only Irish pub, and (2) He wasn't a writer but a *rider*—an unemployed motorcycle racer who had moved to Bend after his San Francisco Kawasaki dealership had gone belly-up.

The moment I got home I called Jillian for an explanation, but I got nothing more than "It was pretty dark and loud in the bar" and "How should I know? The guy was wearing a baseball cap."

As I hung up, I had to wonder, Had Jillian already put me in the category of the desperate? Did she think my only dating criteria were a pulse and a penis? This was all very disturbing.

Thankfully, a couple weeks later, another friend helped set me up with a far more appealing prospect, Bob, a thirty-four-year-old environmental consultant. During a lengthy prescreening by phone, I learned that he was a member of the Bend school board, the parks and rec board, the board of Habitat for Humanity, and the board of Big Brothers and Big Sisters. He was also—and this part was a bit odd for a single, childless guy—a volunteer with the local hospital's "cuddler" program for premature newborns. Despite some misgivings about his overachievement (What was he trying to prove? What void was he trying to fill? When would he find the time to watch *Law & Order* with me?), I couldn't help but admire his sense of social responsibility.

On our first date, a casual lunch, I asked Bob what inspired his passion for volunteering. "I'm a doer!" he said, with the eagerness of a candidate for senior class president. He was cute in a Richie Cunningham kind of way, and I was looking forward to our next date.

The next time, we double-dated with my friends Tom and Susannah at the Bend standby, the bowling alley. In the first frame of the first game, Bob started correcting Tom's technique. "You're releasing too soon," he counseled. "You're not following through." I did not recall Bob mentioning that he volunteered as an instructor on the Pro Bowlers Tour. His senior-class-presidentness was grating on me.

Now, normally, I'm lucky if I can survive an evening of bowling without hurling any gutter balls. But somehow, that night I was transformed, bowling a four-game average of 163 and demolishing my three companions. In the midst of my euphoria, I noticed that the more strikes I threw, the more Bob was giving me the cold shoulder. By the end of the evening, I'd lost all interest in cuddling with the Cuddler.

Over the next few weeks, three acquaintances told me they'd found "the perfect guy" for me. Alas, in all three cases, the guy turned out to be the Cuddler. I was now fearing the worst—that Bend's well of single men was running dry.

It's not like I hadn't had other clues that Bend's demographics weren't exactly working in my favor. The town fairly teemed with retirees, seventeen-year-old snowboarders, and alarmingly young married couples. Once, at the video store, I saw a pregnant woman and her husband, both of whom looked to be in their early twenties, and I thought they seemed awfully young to be starting a family. Then three small children emerged from the animated-film aisle and ran up to the woman shouting, "Mommy!" Back in L.A., I didn't even know anyone who'd given birth before age thirty-two.

The ski group I'd joined turned out to be made up entirely of retired women in their fifties. The third week, I dropped one of my fifty-dollar fleece-lined gloves down the Porta Potti at the snow park, and I was forced to borrow a cheap spare pair from our instructor. My fingers had frozen and my teeth were chattering loudly when one of the ladies looked at me and said, "What you need is a hot flash!" Menopause humor I did not need. All things considered, I chose not to go back.

My gyms hadn't provided any prospects, either. Once I brought a criminal-defense attorney friend along for a workout at one club. "Half the guys in there have felony records," she reported afterward. "I've represented four of them myself. You're at the wrong gym." At this point, it was my only gym. I'd already quit the club with no sight lines.

At this point, almost a year after I'd set off in search of my new home, the novelty of Bend had worn off, and I knew no amount of ginger peach smoothies would bring it back. I reflected on the extensive research I'd done circa Lollapasuza and grasped that there had been a fatal flaw in my plan. I had investigated the weather, the bike trails, the gyms, the coffeehouses, and the cost of living, but I had failed to consider the one question my mother had asked prior to my move: Were there any single men in Bend? While modeling myself after Mary Tyler Moore, I'd forgotten that Mary had remained single the entire run of the show.

It was, to say the least, an unwelcome revelation. I thought about all the months I'd spent struggling over whether to call it quits with Alec. And here I was, a year later, faced with an almost identical issue: How do you know when it's time to break up with an entire town? Like before, I wasn't going to make any rash decisions. I thought about all the effort I'd put into selling myself—not to mention my family and friends—on my new life. I considered all the time and hope I'd invested in the town. And, of course, there was my soft, silky hair. I wasn't ready to let go. Not yet.

Besides, I had something else far more pressing to focus on: preparation for the Death Ride.

Now, I'm sure you've heard the adage that recovering from a breakup takes half as long as the relationship lasted. Alec and I were together thirty-eight months, so technically I still had seven months to get over him before being considered a Really Annoying Person Who Needs to Get a Life. But since Alec seemed to have gotten over me in about seven minutes, I made it a personal challenge to speed up the process.

I knew the only way to be certain I had purged Alec from my system was to actually see him in the flesh. Since I was certain he would be at the Death Ride, it seemed the perfect opportunity. Aside from that, I'd always gotten a lot of satisfaction from the Death Ride, and I wasn't ready to abandon it to him just because we were no longer together. This was my chance to claim as my own what was once "our" event. I relished the idea of spotting him as I pedaled along, offering him a nod, perhaps a little wave, and a coolly civilized "How's it going?" And that would be that.

I knew none of it would be easy. I was in lousy cycling

shape, having barely taken my bike out of the garage during Bend's cold winter, but I was convinced that the distance between me and my I'm Over Him certification was
sixteen thousand vertical feet of pedaling.

"What are you, like a complete fucking masochist?"
Nancy said when I told her of my plans. "First, you choose
the Death Ride to break up with him—and now this? Can't
you find other ways to torture yourself? Don't they have
Death Rides in Oregon?"

But I would have none of it. "Look, do you want me to
be over him or not?" I said. And besides, I thought, there were
those great ice cream sandwiches at the top of the last pass.

I got a late start on my drive, four hundred miles of bar-
ren highway with only two towns along the way, and knew
I'd have to spend the night on the road. I was drowsy and
already a bit anxious by the time I pulled into the second
town—Alturas, California—and stopped at the first motel I
saw, the Drifter's Inn. I checked in with the German teenager at the front desk and rushed to my room to call Nancy
for moral support.

This was when I discovered that I had not merely traveled to the northeasternmost corner of California; I had
traveled back in time. My room had a rotary telephone. I
examined it for a while, lifting the receiver, placing my fingertips in the dial holes, feeling like I had excavated a woolly
mammoth tusk. I then dialed zero and had the following
conversation:

Operator:	Citizens Telephone, may I help you?
Me:	Yes, I would like to make a credit-card call.
Operator:	You'll need an AT&T operator for that, ma'am.

Me: Well, who are you?

Operator: I'm a Citizens Telephone operator.

Me: But you're still an operator, right? Don't operators help people make credit-card calls?

Operator: I can't do that for you, ma'am. But I'll patch you through to AT&T.

(The next thing I hear is a busy signal. I call the operator back.)

Me: It's me again. I don't understand—I got a busy signal. How is it possible that an entire telephone company is busy?

Operator: I have no idea, ma'am, but I'll try patching you through again.

After several more attempts, I realized my irritation far exceeded my need to hear any words of reassurance from Nancy, so I gave up and went to sleep.

Because I had waited until the last minute to book a motel room near the Death Ride, I was forced to stay the next night in Carson City, Nevada, a full hour from the starting line. Upon arriving at my motel, I asked the desk clerk to schedule my wakeup call for 3 A.M., calculating that would give me enough time to eat at Denny's en route and start pedaling at 5:15. The clerk asked me three times whether I actually meant 3 P.M. before shrugging and shooting me a look that said, "Okay, you crazy lady."

Between my worry that he'd gotten the time wrong and a growing anxiety over what the next day would bring, I lay awake all night and was dressed in my cycling gear long before the wakeup call came. I was hardly rested, but I figured packing away a zillion carbs at breakfast would give me the head start I needed. At 3:45, I arrived at Denny's only to learn an astonishing fact: Denny's is *not* always open. This was almost as shocking as learning there were still rotary telephones in use. Wasn't "Always Open" the Denny's motto? Didn't the company advertise that fact on national television? If they had changed their policy, weren't they obligated to inform the public?

My stomach was starting to grumble when I remembered a nearby casino where Alec and I had eaten before—surely it was open. I arrived at 4:03 and sat down at the counter next to a guy dressed in a Death Ride jersey and cycling tights. He was working on three fried eggs, hash browns, four strips of bacon, and a large stack of pancakes dripping with maple syrup and butter. I was ready to place the same order when the waitress said, "Sorry, hon, the grill's closed from four to five, but I can get you some cereal."

When I realized she wasn't kidding, panic set in. I knew the only place to buy food between the casino and the starting line was a Chevron station. I knew that I would not reach the first Death Ride food stop until 7 A.M., at which point it would be way, way too late to start fueling my muscles for a twelve-hour ride. I stuffed down all the corn flakes I could, but there was no denying reality: I was in deep shit.

With sunrise still an hour away, I sped to the course in a state of alarm. I was in the worst shape of my cycling career. I was about to see my ex-boyfriend. And I was famished. This was nuts. All I had to do was turn the car around, start back to Bend, and it would be over. I could go on with my life as if I'd never even had this loony idea. But my hands stayed steady on the wheel. I just couldn't bear the idea of quitting before I'd even started. As I slowed down to look for a parking spot, I wondered when I would run out of energy, when I would run into Alec, and which would happen first.

My answer arrived shortly: Alec passed me near the top of the first mountain pass, with such speed that I felt like I was pedaling backward. "You can do it!" he shouted as he powered ahead. He wasn't taunting me. He was just offering his standard cheer, the one he'd give any struggling cyclist on the mountain. I was so wounded I couldn't even respond. This was the same guy who used to phone me every couple of hours just to hear my voice? The same guy who used to wrap his arms around me as I fell asleep at night? The last of my emotional reserves had vanished somewhere between the casino and the starting line. My goal to earn my I'm Over Him certification was now officially downgraded to Finishing Without Falling to Pieces. Already gasping for breath from the altitude and exhaustion, I was now fighting tears.

Alec passed me on the second climb and again on the third. (He was stopping at each summit to wait for friends, which meant he started every pass behind me and finished ahead.) Lunch was demoralizing. Alec sat with his friends under one tree, and I sat by myself under another. One of his friends waved gamely in my direction.

I won't recount every excruciating detail of the Death Ride. Suffice it to say I was on the course *fourteen and a half* hours, seven of which I spent in such agony that it seemed like even my hair hurt. I was so dizzy and nauseous and so tormented by my throbbing feet and aching back that I had to stop and lie on the side of the road five times on the stretch to the final summit. When I finally rolled into the rest stop, I learned that they'd just run out of ice cream sandwiches.

I would like to report that I completed all 130 miles of the Death Ride, but with only a quarter mile to go, at the base of a small rise, I pulled over to the side of the road and collapsed. A few minutes later, I flagged down a pickup truck and asked for a ride to my car.

"Sure, how far is it?" the driver asked.

"It's right over there," I said, pointing to my Trooper, about four hundred yards in front of us.

The only good thing about the entire day was that Alec was long gone before I reached the end.

When I got to my car, I took off my shoes, sat in the front seat, and sobbed on the steering wheel for twenty solid minutes. I was stunned at how badly I had miscalculated. A good night's sleep, a pep talk from Nancy, a mountain of Denny's pancakes—it wouldn't have mattered. I was in no condition, physically or emotionally, to have put myself through this kind of torture.

It took me eleven hours to drive the four hundred miles back to Bend because I stopped so many times to rest. Just outside of Alturas, I was pulled over by the California Highway Patrol for reckless driving. I pointed to my bike and pleaded exhaustion, and the officer let me off with a warning once I promised to pull over and take a nap before I killed myself or someone else. I stopped at a park and slept for three hours under a tree.

I returned to Bend drained and cranky, and things spiraled downward from there. Over the next few weeks, my laundry piled up. My bills went unpaid. At Hebrew class I snapped at a fellow student who kept pronouncing the guttural "ch" sound as if it were a "k."

I knew, deep down, that there was only one thing to do: move back to L.A. I needed to regroup. I missed my friends. I missed the familiar places. I missed the opportunity to see movies besides *Alien* and *Scream II*. Besides, in L.A., the demographics were in my favor. The city was home to seven million men.

I gave notice on my pine-trimmed house. "I hope you don't feel like your experiment was a failure," said my landlord, Doug. It was a sweet sentiment, but failure is what I felt. I blamed only myself, not Bend. It would have been a delightful place to live—if I hadn't been single.

Still, at the same time, I felt a huge weight lifted off my shoulders. I didn't have to be the New Girl in Town anymore. I could just go back to being me. I called my family and friends to announce that I was coming home.

"Now you're using your head," Grandpa said. "Bend is yesterday's newspaper."

"I'll make you an appointment with Angela," my sister said, referring to her high-priced hairdresser, who would, presumably, be equipped to deal with the frizz problems that surely awaited me.

My parents were so thrilled that they threw themselves into the task of finding me an appropriately appointed apartment.

For once, Nancy kept her commentary succinct. "Mazel tov," she said.

Day 1400
B.C.E.

Day 1
C.E.

Day 1000
C.E.

11

The E-Male of My Dreams

I was already beginning to tie up my loose ends around Bend when Nancy called back a few days later with some news that made me feel even better about coming home. A friend of hers in L.A. had found the perfect boyfriend using a new Internet dating service called match.com. "Check it out," Nancy urged.

This was back in the early days of Internet dating, long before match.com became to singles what Costco is to soccer moms. In fact, it was the first time I'd even heard of it. But once I logged on for my free preview, I thought the idea was brilliant.

For a small monthly fee, you could post your vital info, which would then be perused by the opposite sex. Photos were optional, but most members had them. Instantly, you could read, in detail, how the guys described themselves and their ideal match, how they felt about religion, music, politics, television—a major improvement over newspaper personal ads, which gave you little to go on besides "SWM seeks SWF for LTR." With the click of a mouse, you could screen out men who smoked or didn't want to have children or lived more than twenty-five miles from your ZIP code. And with a glance at the essays and a few anonymous e-mail exchanges, you could easily pick the cream of the crop. The photos even eliminated the surprise element with appearance.

The whole thing sounded so practical, not to mention efficient. What an incredible amount of time and agony it would save! Never again would I end up with guys like the LHP or the LHJ or the Cuddler. There would be no more bland insurance brokers or writer/rider mix-ups. Match.com was the one missing tool I needed to be in control of my own destiny.

I did worry a little that my friends might think my new strategy had the whiff of desperation, but when Kate phoned me later that day and I told her what I was doing, she had a different concern. "Won't this take all the romance out it?" she asked. "It's kind of like getting pregnant through in vitro fertilization instead of the old-fashioned way. Sure, the outcome's the same, but still . . ." I completely disagreed and told her so. Plucking your true love out of thin air—what could be more romantic than that?

Even though I wouldn't be moving for a month, I decided to get a jump start on the process. With luck, maybe I'd even have a few dates waiting for me when I pulled into town. For just a $14.95 investment, I was buying back what had waned in Bend: hope. There was no doubt in my mind I would find someone. And soon.

I posted my photo, taken in Bend so no frizz was apparent, along with a succinct profile crafted to suggest a girl who didn't take herself too seriously ("low-maintenance

traveler, *Spinal Tap* worshipper, loyal friend, lousy cook . . .").
I detailed what I was looking for in a guy ("thoughtful,
funny, athletic, spontaneous, not a workaholic"), and listed
my "likes" (cycling, Scrabble, country music, guys who
remember your birthday) and "dislikes" (pets, men with
ponytails). Real names, of course, weren't used, so I picked
as my handle "Fitwriter." Not only was it literal and to the
point, but it also distinguished me from all the screen names
like "Hottie4u" and "Only1forUbabe."

The first day, my criteria matched thirty-three guys. I
was elated. The number alone suggested I was well on my
way to ending my dry spell, now thirteen months and
counting. For comparison's sake, I did a search from my
Bend ZIP code and came up with just one match within a
fifty-mile radius—an LHT, long-haired teacher. It was just
more evidence that I was headed in the right direction.

However, my euphoria was tempered once I actually
read the essays and realized a significant percentage of these
guys fell into several less-than-enticing categories.

The most common match.com man appeared to be the
Drip, a guy who seemed to harbor almost a burning desire
to be uninteresting. His essay was typified by three telltale
characteristics: (1) a *Cops*-style physical description ("I am
a single white male, 5'11", 165 pounds, brown hair, hazel
eyes."), (2) a stupefyingly dull account of his life ("I have a
home in Gardena and work for a small company in
Cerritos. I'm an electrical engineer that designs electrical
systems. Because it is a small company, I am involved in
many different aspects, including sales, marketing, and customer support. I grew up in Iowa and moved to Nebraska
for college. Well, I guess that's about all for now."), and (3)
clichés that seemed to be passed verbatim from one Drip

essay to the next like a virus ("I like romantic walks on the beach and sunsets. I like a girl who likes to laugh and likes to have fun.")

Then there was the match.com Egomaniac, the guy who fully expected every woman to drop to her knees and weep openly at his wonderfulness (no doubt right before giving him a blow job). His essay tended to come in one of two styles, either (1) shameless conceit (from InvestInMe: "I recently paid off my new five-bedroom home and am well on my way to being a millionaire") or (2) shameless conceit unsuccessfully disguised as humility (from MalibuDan: "I'm often asked if I'm a model or an actor, but I'm more the writer/intellectual type").

Less prevalent, thankfully, was a category of guys who didn't so much turn me off as just give me the creeps—the Norman Bates of match.com. Exhibit No. 1 was Jim555: "You sound like my dream girl. I'm 57, 5'5", ex-Air Force. I am living in Fallon, Nevada, with my mother of seventy-four on what used to be a farm." (This was the e-mail that prompted me to abandon a short-lived policy of answering all match.com responses out of courtesy.) Exhibit No. 2 was ICUDB4U, a Santa Monica attorney who wrote me two hours after I received his first e-mail: "Didn't you get my last e-mail? Why haven't you responded?? Was it something I said?"

As I sorted through my "matches" and began receiving e-mails from other members, I was beginning to sense that a love connection might take a bit more time than I had initially expected. But then remarkably, after just three days, BikeMan surfaced on my screen. "You sound really cool!" he wrote, introducing himself as a serious cyclist who worked in advertising.

For the next couple of days, BikeMan and I volleyed e-mails, discovering all sorts of similarities besides our interest in riding a bike. Both Jewish, we'd grown up a few miles apart and attended single-sex prep schools, and we had the same favorite game, Boggle. BikeMan seemed to be an intriguing bundle of contradictions: a guy who'd go for a killer seventy-mile ride, then spend the afternoon at a sculpture exhibit; a software programmer who didn't own a home computer. "I really enjoy writing letters and reading by candlelight and listening to the radio in a very low-tech, early-century sort of way," he wrote.

Our e-mails soon drifted below the surface. He wrote to me about his absent father and his needy ex-girlfriend. I told him about Alec and my downward spiral in Bend. BikeMan seemed to possess the very qualities—sensitivity and self-awareness—that Alec so glaringly lacked. "It sounds like you went through some emotional turbulence when you went your separate way most recently," he wrote. "What do you miss the most? What are you glad you left behind?"

BikeMan hadn't posted his picture on match.com, and I hadn't asked to see one for fear he'd think I was superficial. But I swiftly decided the issue was moot, as he began reeling me in with e-mails that were lyrical, literate, and provocative. "The best poets," he wrote, "are like the best journalists: They have extraordinary powers of perception and description." Quite a contrast, this was, to Alec's writing: "Victim stated that suspect was wearing red hooded jacket."

By the time BikeMan and I had exchanged dozens of e-mails, I felt like we were in a genuine dating relationship but without the complications—deciding on meeting places, making nervous small talk, constantly worrying if he's feeling what you're feeling. Even better, our next date was just a click away. In fact, e-dating was so easy that I found myself in the throes of that first-flutter compulsion to be together all the time. And without the barriers of time and place, we almost could. The only thing missing, of course, was the actual flesh, but I was certain that would come.

After about a week, BikeMan sent me a picture out of the blue. He had a full head of light brown curly hair and an endearing smile, and though I wasn't bowled over, by then I was so enamored with him that his looks didn't matter. Instinct told me that we were an extraordinary match.

I suppose I'm the one who nudged our e-mails into X-rated territory. After so many emotionally intimate exchanges, I was convinced BikeMan and I would sleep together sooner or later, and I was hoping for sooner, especially considering I hadn't had sex in more than a year. But, I had to know, did he feel the same way? I debated for a couple of days about how to broach the subject without risking embarrassment if he wasn't interested (all the while grateful that e-mail gave me the opportunity to be so calculating). Then the perfect line came to me—a casual remark made on the pretext of describing my day.

"So I had the longest wait at the gynecologist this morning," I wrote, "and while I was sitting there, I figured out that I've spent more than $400 on birth control pills that haven't gone to any use."

Less than ten minutes later, I had my reply. "Fear not," BikeMan said. "Everyone has some underutilized product from time to time. Got some decomposing latex myself."

He'd bit! With the word "latex," there was no turning back. Soon we were discussing likes and dislikes—and I don't mean country music and ponytails.

I'd never imagined I was someone who could participate in cybersex—wasn't that the sort of person who wrote in to *Penthouse* "Forum"?—but the next thing I knew, BikeMan and I were trading torrid e-mails so furiously that I couldn't get any work done. During my final week in Bend, I was walking around with an ear-to-ear grin. One afternoon a woman I barely knew stopped me on the street and said, "You look radiant today!"

Once I broke the news about BikeMan to my cabinet, reaction was split. The "Are You Insane?" faction tended to be the married ones. "I just worry that you're setting yourself up for disappointment," said Dana, the cabinet member who usually was the first to look for the bright side. "Besides, how do you know that he's not the next Ted Bundy?"

The "You Go, Girl!" contingent included people like my San Francisco friend Sarah, who had already discovered the seductive power of the Internet. Several months before, she had struck up a romance with a lawyer in Chicago whom she'd "met" through business e-mail correspondence. At the time, I thought she'd lost all common sense, if not her mind. But then, after they'd exchanged steamy e-mails for a month, he hopped a plane to visit her. They had great sex and felt an amazing connection, and four months later, she moved in with him in Chicago for a trial run. They'd since moved back to San Francisco and now were practically engaged. Okay, I thought, maybe she wasn't crazy, but surely this was a fluke.

Now, with BikeMan in the picture, I understood completely. You really could get to know someone through e-mail—more deeply and honestly, perhaps, than you could in person. As our romance heated up and my move date neared, we started planning our first rendezvous. Certainly, it would involve sex. "Won't that ruin the potential for a long-term relationship?" Dana asked, forsaking her usual optimism. I told her I felt like we'd been dating for weeks and at this point, sex was only natural. BikeMan agreed.

The two of us debated about whether we should talk on the phone before meeting. We worried that a conversation might ruin the momentum we'd generated via e-mail. But finally we decided we couldn't wait any longer, so we set up a phone date the night before I left Bend.

The conversation was incredible. No awkward silences, no regrettable missteps. We talked for two hours with complete ease.

"I feel like I just won the lottery," he said shortly before we hung up.

"I know what you mean," I replied. "I feel the same way."

I left Bend feeling as cheerful as the day I had arrived. I marveled at how quickly I had rebounded—from the Death Ride debacle, from the depths of my despair. As I drove out of town, the weather was unusually damp, and lightning flashed in the sky. My hair expanded—yet another sign that it was time for me to go. At a truck stop in central California I bought BikeMan a lottery ticket. I couldn't wait to give it to him.

Day 1400
B.C.E.

Day 1
C.E.

Day 1000
C.E.

12

The BikeMan Cometh

*Y*ou know when you were a kid and it was your birthday and there was this humongous pile of presents with your name on them and all you could think about was tearing open the wrapping and ripping into the boxes and getting your hands on what you were certain was your dream collection of Superstar Barbie accessories? But you couldn't open the gifts because first you had to endure the party— the miniature golf or the bowling or the pottery decorating or whatever drudgery your parents had drummed up in order to assure you the giant haul of presents. The whole time you were putting or painting clay mugs, all you could think about were the presents. The presents! I want my presents!

Well, that's pretty much how I felt on my first day back in L.A., the day I was going to meet BikeMan, the man of my dreams, my future husband, my tall, sexy, curly-haired welcome-home present. I couldn't think of anything else but him—in various stages of undress, in various positions, in various rooms in the fabulous new Spanish-style apartment my sister had found for me. But I had to stifle all of my energy and excitement because first I had to get through the morning and afternoon with my family, engaged in the activity that they most thrive on, succeed at, and indeed live for: unpacking.

Whenever any member of my family relocates, there is no transition period involving boxes in the corner or suitcases on the floor. Within hours, dishes are stacked, books are shelved, suits are hung (on wooden hangers), candle snuffers are displayed. My family operates on the premise that, at any given moment, *Architectural Digest* might call to request an emergency photo shoot.

Personally, I operate on the premise that, at any given moment, there might be something really good on TV and that the unpacking process should involve frequent rest breaks to play with the remote. Left to my own devices, I would live out of boxes for weeks, if not months. And certainly, in this case, I would have invited BikeMan over first thing in the morning, boxes be damned. But I could hardly reject my family's offer to help me settle in, since (1) that would have been ungracious, and (2) I didn't want to tell them about my new boyfriend for at least a few weeks, for fear they'd join the "Are You Insane?" faction.

First to arrive for unpacking duty were my parents. Mom organized the kitchen while Dad filled the place with plants and flowers, including a pink orchid to match the tile in my bathroom. Jen arrived later with her boyfriend, John, whom she'd started dating around the time I moved to Bend. I'd met him only once, on a visit home, and I'd instantly liked him, even though he was an LHA (long-haired actor). He had a wry sense of humor and was easy to talk to, and I could see that he and Jen complemented each other well. John's tendency to wear Metallica concert T-shirts was balanced by Jen's talent for finding bargains at Barneys; her various moods were balanced by his unflappable nature. John also had an amazing capacity to tune out my family's peculiarities, no doubt honed from his years as a substitute teacher at inner-city high schools, where students referred to him as "Mr. Weird," "Mr. Queer," and "Shawn Michaels" (at the time, a popular LHPW—long-haired professional wrestler).

By the time of my return to L.A., John had already earned rave reviews from my parents and grandparents. He permanently endeared himself to me the day of the move by devoting eight straight hours to emptying boxes, breaking them down, and transporting them to the trash. Plus, he didn't think I was odd when I asked him to take the Iron Photo— the commemorative photograph, shot each time I moved, of me holding the box containing my iron. I'd never actually used this iron, a housewarming gift circa my first apartment, and six moves later it remained sealed in its original box.

My sister, meanwhile, focused on helping me arrange the furniture. The rugs, tables, and lamps I'd bought in Bend worked remarkably well in my new place, although Jen did order me to destroy the candles covered in pine bark. "Enough with the pine," she said. "We're over it."

Even though I'd left there only a couple days before, it struck me that I was just as finished with Bend. What I'd once thought was my permanent destination now seemed like a mere transition, a place where I'd gone to recuperate from my breakup with Alec. The whole Death Ride experience seemed to have purged him from my system, and I'd realized as I recounted the whole story to BikeMan in my e-mails that Alec was history. Now I was back where I belonged, primed for my real life, which no doubt would be starting that evening. Sure, my rent had doubled, my new street had a two-hour parking limit, and the neighborhood was clogged with traffic, but none of that mattered. I had a boyfriend, and I was going to have sex!

By the time I shooed my family out the door so I could get dressed for his arrival, the only task remaining was to hang some artwork. All in all, my apartment was going to look phenomenal for BikeMan.

Of course, I hoped to look phenomenal, too. I picked out a tight white tank top and a loose print skirt. Getting dressed, I was so jumpy that I tripped on the skirt and landed on my knees. My hair did what it wanted to do, given that I hadn't yet had my consultation with Angela. I took the lottery ticket out of my wallet and put it in the drawer of my nightstand for just the right moment.

At six on the dot, the doorbell rang. I smoothed my hair, took a deep breath, and opened the door to my new future. There, on the other side, stood a skinny, gawky fellow wearing an oversized yellow T-shirt, dark jeans, and a goofy grin. *This* was BikeMan?

My heart felt like it had been hit by a wrecking ball. Where was the strapping, poetic e-male of my fantasies? What had this guy done with him? The picture just didn't compute. BikeMan had claimed to be five-foot-ten, three inches taller than me, but in person he appeared to be barely my height. He'd mentioned he was thin—"wiry" was the word he'd used—but now he appeared to be drowning in his clothes. This was the guy with whom I'd exchanged everything but bodily fluids?

BikeMan offered a sweeping gesture that said, "Ta-da!"

Mustering all my reserves to conceal my disappointment and distress, I gave him a hug and took the Turkish pastries he'd brought as a housewarming gift. But as we made small talk in the kitchen, my mind was racing. Who was this guy, anyway? What had I gotten myself into? Had I just made a colossal mistake? Could I politely back out of the sex we'd planned? Did I really want to back out? Would he grow on me? How could he possibly grow on me? Was I, deep down, a shallow, judgmental bitch?

The last question gave me considerable pause. Could I really be that hung up on looks? But then I took a reality check: Wasn't I the one who had a semicrush on Hank Goldberg, the bookish, pasty member of the O.J. prosecution team? No, this wasn't about appearance. BikeMan really wasn't a bad-looking fellow. The issue here was about attraction, that involuntary primal response that makes your heart race and your palms sweat. This is not something you can control. Standing there in the kitchen, I was feeling nothing close to primal for BikeMan.

Meanwhile, BikeMan seemed oblivious to my agony. He even appeared to be enjoying himself, but then, I didn't know him well enough to tell if he was pretending just like me. As we continued to chat, I knew I had to do something. But what?

I assessed the situation. Fact: I had not had sex in fourteen months. Fact: I had a willing and able partner twenty feet from my bedroom. But was a starved libido a good enough reason to get naked with a guy I really didn't want to see naked?

Of course, there was another reason to consider: guilt. BikeMan and I had had a deal. I couldn't exactly back out on him now. After all our e-mail soul-baring, I wasn't so brazen as to risk hurting his feelings. And so, a half hour after his arrival, I took his hand and led him into the bedroom.

The sex, in the narrowest sense, was great. We had, after all, memorized each other's playbooks. But everything else felt wrong. I simply could not connect the guy I'd envisioned with the guy in my bed. When the flesh-and-blood BikeMan uttered the same phrases that his online counterpart had used, I felt like he was stealing the other guy's lines, like he was some kind of imposter.

In my fantasies, I had imagined that after sex, the two of us would lie in a tender embrace for hours, gazing into each other's eyes, marveling at our good fortune. At just the right moment, I'd pull out the lottery ticket and present it to him, and we'd both chuckle over our little private joke. But now I was beginning to grasp reality: BikeMan and I were strangers. Whether that would change in the future remained to be seen, but at the moment I just wanted to get out from under the sheets. The whole lottery ticket scene, of course, was now on the cutting-room floor.

Not knowing what to say or do next, I jumped in the shower. Then, while BikeMan was showering, my doorbell rang. I couldn't imagine who would be showing up unannounced—my friends didn't even have my new address. My hair still wrapped in a towel, I opened the door and found my sister and a friend of hers.

"I wanted to show Vanessa your amazing new apartment!" Jen said.

"Hi!" I said, my mind searching frantically for even the feeblest excuse to get rid of them as they walked right in.

"Um, there's a guy in my shower—I'll explain later!" I blurted out just as BikeMan, his wet curls dripping onto his yellow T-shirt, wandered into the living room and cheerfully introduced himself. I was simultaneously mortified and relieved to have the break. Now, BikeMan and I wouldn't have to discuss the events that had just transpired. For the next hour and a half, the four of us—my sister, Vanessa, BikeMan, and I—hung photographs around my apartment. I did manage to telegraph the headlines of my predicament to Jen through rolled eyes and furrowed brows, and I was confident that she would keep this episode to herself around the family.

After Jen and Vanessa left, BikeMan and I went out for a late dinner, and the vibe continued to be strange. It didn't really feel like a first date, but neither did it feel like a second or a fifth or a tenth. Considering the massive volume of e-mail we'd exchanged, the secrets we'd shared, and the fact that we'd already had sex, I never anticipated sitting across the table from him asking, "So, have you seen any good movies lately?" and "Do you think the Democrats will win back the House?" The Internet had turned centuries-old dating protocol upside down.

Ours wasn't the kind of panicky awkwardness you feel after having sex with a friend (which you handle with furtive assurances that nothing has changed). It wasn't the blasé awkwardness you feel after sex with someone you only met hours before (which you deal with by getting dressed and saying, "Well, see ya," as you walk out the door). This was just plain weird awkwardness. I'd invested all this time and emotion, but it turned out to be for someone who existed only in cyberspace. As for BikeMan, I had no clue how he felt, and I wasn't sure I wanted to know.

BikeMan didn't spend the night, not that it was even a possibility. I did not yet have a parking permit for guests and was suddenly grateful for L.A.'s perennial shortage of spaces. Anyway, I needed time to sort things out. On the one hand, BikeMan and I had a lot in common, and I had felt a deep connection with him via e-mail. On the other hand, I was racked with guilt and confusion over the lack of attraction. But struggling through this, I saw there was only one thing I knew for certain: I wanted more sex.

True, this response sent me hurtling toward the classically male territory of "Who wants love when you can get laid?" But at this point I was utterly incredulous that I'd had to wait more than a year to have sex. Even among the testosterone-challenged, something happens to you when you've been deprived of sex that long and are then given a less-than-ideal version. Your first reaction isn't, "Thanks, fella. Now I'll be off to search for Mr. Right." No way. Not when every one of your erogenous zones have just been shaken awake and are now howling for more.

The next day, I called my friends to catch them up on my latest chapter and gauge opinion. Nobody said, "Dump him."

"You can't judge people on first impressions," said Nancy.

"Don't blow it—you've got to give him more of a chance," said Cristina, an artist in Bend who was the most recent addition to my cabinet. Cristina, who was happily married, reminded me that when she first met the man who was to become her husband, she was "totally not interested" in him.

"Get as much sex out of it as you can," said Sarah, who'd lived through a fairly long dry spell before meeting the Internet guy she was now practically engaged to.

That night, I had dinner with my family at a Chinese restaurant, and my fortune said, "Don't let doubt and suspicion bar your progress." I would have taken it as a sign except that I wasn't sure what it was trying to say. Should I ignore my doubts about BikeMan and give the relationship time to develop? Or should I stop feeling guilty, have more sex, and then give him the heave-ho?

Awash with rationalizations, I decided to proceed with caution and give it a go with BikeMan, who didn't seem to be doing any equivocating, which made me feel even more guilty. I did try to bring up how we felt about each other, but he suggested we not analyze whatever we had and just start spending time together fully clothed. But that was the problem. Try as I might, I couldn't see us as a couple anywhere except the bedroom. Within a week, I was arranging my schedule so that going out was nearly an impossibility. "I'll be over there at ten after a movie with some friends," I would call to tell him, "but I can't stay over because I've got to get up at six to ride." I was usually gone by midnight.

BikeMan did all the things that should have endeared him to me. He laughed at my jokes. He bought me a great pair of earrings. He told me funny stories about his neighbors. But it was clear we had no chemistry. Retreating to traditional female turf, I decided that sex without it was worse than no sex at all (although had I known this would be the start of the Streak, I might have hung in there a little longer). A month after our first offline encounter, I told BikeMan that I'd had fun but felt we just weren't a match. He said he'd sensed my waning interest, gave me a hug, then darted out the door.

I was overcome with relief—so much so that it really didn't matter I was saying good-bye to a guy I'd once thought would be the great love of my life. Although some friends had worried that I'd set myself up for a huge fall, the crash didn't happen. Investing emotionally online, it turned out, wasn't much of an investment at all.

C.E.

(The Celibacy Era)

Sex is like air; it's not important unless you aren't getting any.

—Unknown

Day 1400
B.C.E.

Day 1
C.E.

Day 1000
C.E.

13

Blind Trust

So I'd had it all wrong. I could now see that you can't properly evaluate a potential boyfriend by the way he writes e-mail, no matter how lyrical, literate, or provocative. Without face time, there's no foolproof way to detect a spark. And isn't that where real attraction starts—that immediate spark? You need eye contact to sense if something has lit up inside that could lead to chemical combustion. Alec was evidence enough that in-person sparkness was what really mattered. He wrote entire arrest warrants without a single comma and thought "diluted" and "deluded" were the same word. (Me: "You're so deluded"; him: "I'm watered down?") If I'd met him online, I'd have hit "delete," and I'd have missed out on a relationship that, I saw in retrospect, had that spark.

Sure, my friend Sarah had found true love online. She was even grateful she'd met her boyfriend over the Internet; if they'd been introduced at a party, she said, she'd have dismissed him because he wasn't her usual type. But now I was certain Sarah's experience was a fluke.

After BikeMan, I decided to give myself a breather on the dating front, get going on some new work assignments, and just enjoy my new start in L.A. For the first time, I didn't curse the traffic or the long lines at Baja Fresh. They existed because L.A. had something Bend did not: millions and millions of people.

I didn't need to join organizations or temples or classes, because now I had an actual social life. I reconnected with friends, a few of whom were also single, and we went to movies or out to eat. No longer did I have to run off to Nairobi to have a conversation with someone who really knew me. I felt like the old me again, or maybe a new version of the old me, or maybe a newer version of the new me. Whatever it was, it felt good. I knew it was only a matter of time before I came across a guy with spark potential.

About a month after the move, I signed back onto match.com, determined to employ a new strategy. I still believed in the brilliance of the Web site as a screening tool. I just had to correct a rookie mistake. No more lengthy e-mails or preliminary phone conversations. If I saw anything that caught my eye—say, "athletic" or "*Spinal Tap* fan"— I figured it was good enough to seek a face-to-face meeting. And rather than plan dinner dates or outings about town, I would increase the efficiency of the screening process by heading straight for Starbucks. If sparks flew, we could always plan a real date. If the meeting was a bust, well, we'd have only cost ourselves forty-five minutes and the price of a Frappuccino.

I viewed these coffee dates as predates, not unlike the process of getting preapproved for a loan: You cover a short list of questions, and you know whether it's thumbs-up or -down before having to go through the whole rigamarole. With virtually nothing at stake, I figured, I wouldn't show up nervous or come away disappointed, distressed, or guilt-ridden.

I tried out my new tack on Philly1962, who said he was "in health care" and enjoyed lifting weights. Our correspondence, in its entirety:

> Me: Hi, sounds like we have some things in common—want to meet for coffee?
>
> Philly: Sure, where/when?
>
> Me: Starbucks, Encino, Thurs., noon.
>
> Philly: Okay, see ya then.

As I expected, I felt little anxiety walking into Starbucks, where I found Philly at the counter struggling to read the board as if it were written in Middle English.

"So, what exactly is a mocha?" he asked, explaining he preferred to consume all food and beverages in the comfort of his own home. Philly, a pudgier version of his online photo, had worked in the accounting department of the same health-insurance company for nineteen years and was about to be given an entire year's severance pay because the company was being bought out.

"Wow, what an amazing opportunity to do new things and travel!" I said.

"Oh, geez," he said in such a way that I knew the idea had never crossed his mind. "At first I thought I might take a few weeks off, but that seems too risky. So I'm going to find another job while I still have one and then take a week to visit my cousins in Ohio."

Philly said he lifted weights at home because going to a gym would interfere with his "routine," which consisted of going to work, coming home for lunch, going back to work, cooking dinner, doing laundry, and ironing. "To take an hour to go to the gym—I just can't see where I'd find the time," he said.

Philly and I were no match for any number of reasons, not the least of which was his commitment to ironing. But the get-together did confirm how much easier it was to extricate yourself from a bad predate than from a bad real date. Gone was all the tedious blather while you—or maybe both of you—tried to think of a polite escape line. Not that rudeness was acceptable on a predate, but it struck me as perfectly okay to cut off the conversation at any point by saying, "Well, hey, I've got some errands to run. It was nice to meet you—good luck with that job hunt!"

I chalked up the Philly experience to bad luck rather than any flaw in my approach. I mean, what were the odds that I was going to end up in bed with the first *two* guys I met through match.com? But after a few more dead-end insta-dates—including one with a guy who claimed to be a professional writer but turned out to be a security guard who wrote sci-fi screenplays while working the graveyard shift at a Bel Air mansion—I did start to wonder whether my new strategy needed some refinements. I was a little shocked that the security guard had had the nerve to embellish. I mean, did he really think bait and switch worked with dating? (Though friends out of the Internet-dating loop assumed most people exaggerate in their profiles, most of the guys I met were pretty much as they described.)

Meanwhile, I was discovering a few more facets to the downside of living within miles of my family. For the previous four years—three in Berkeley, one in Bend—I'd become accustomed to conducting my life as I pleased, with minimal scrutiny from my parents and grandparents. I could drive to Winnemucca and back without anyone realizing that I'd ever left the house. I could go dateless for weeks, if not months, and simply filter the information I provided. ("Oh, I'm meeting lots of people—things are going fine!") But Jen's impromptu visit was just the beginning.

In those first few months back home, my calendar filled up fast with family gatherings—dinners, weekend brunches, birthdays, anniversaries, and holiday celebrations. My sister always brought John. My cousin came with her fiancé. When talk inevitably turned to their wedding plans or to the upcoming wedding of another cousin, who lived in Berkeley, my singleness was now standing out like a giant zit on the end of my nose.

Actually, it was worse than that because when you have a giant zit, people go out of their way to pretend it isn't there. But the more time my family spent around me, the less shy they became about bringing up the subject of my single state. At one family dinner, Grandpa barked, "Suzanne, haven't you met any guys yet? You've been back here four months now." I hadn't realized anyone was counting.

Not long after that, my parents hauled me out to dinner, alone, and handed me literature for a Jewish volunteer organization aimed at singles ages twenty-five to forty. I felt like a drug addict trapped in an intervention.

Although my parents did, eventually, respond to requests like, "Can we *please* not discuss this?" I had no such luck with my grandparents, who seemed convinced that nothing they said would be heard unless they repeated it at least 150 times.

Not only were Grandma Honey and Grandpa Julius unafraid to keep mentioning my singleness, but they were also completely oblivious to how obstinate both had become in countless other ways. They refused to set foot in any movie theater where they were not already "familiar with the restroom facilities"—an edict that reduced their options to a single multiplex, one that had recently begun to specialize in violent action films. The night we saw *Enemy of the State,* Grandpa fell asleep and Grandma walked out after thirty minutes and sat in the lobby for the duration. But afterward, they staunchly defended their movie choice. "I knew exactly where to find the restroom," Grandma said, adding that she had used it twice and it needed a good cleaning.

Meanwhile, I was spending Saturday afternoons playing Scrabble with Grandma Ruth, whose health, sadly, was rapidly deteriorating. The only activities that seemed to give her any pleasure were smoking, eating blue Jell-O at the Sizzler ("Well, I'll be darned," she'd remark at every visit. "It's blue!"), and pointing out that I was older than my two engaged cousins. Grandma kept insisting I tell her precisely when I would be walking down the aisle. "Six months?" she'd say in her gravelly voice. "A year?"

Although my grandparents seemed to think I was spending my free time playing darts in my bedroom, in the six months after my return I had actually been making a considerable effort on the dating front. About the time my new match.com strategy fizzled, I began to get the motherlode of setups—as if all my family's friends had been accumulating names, like frequent-flyer miles, in anticipation of my return.

Given my string of disastrous setups in Bend, I did have second thoughts about going that route again. But this time, the people trying to fix me up were friends who'd known me for years, so I figured the odds of a match were much higher. Still, just to be on the safe side, I decided to stick to the Starbucks predate approach. When you get fixed up, you know that the mutual friend who did the fixing will inevitably hear both sides of the story, so you have to be careful if the date ends up a disaster.

My first setup was with a lawyer named David who looked a lot like George Will and showed up at our 10 P.M. date wearing a navy blue suit. He hadn't come from work, he said; he just preferred wearing suits. He told me, in hushed tones, that he was starting an Internet company; but he would not reveal its mission, apparently afraid I might steal his idea. He did mention he was planning to raise five million dollars. "You could say it's a big risk," he said, pausing to grab his lapels, "but I feel really comfortable with it."

I left the date baffled as to why anyone would think David and I were a potential couple, until I realized: Our mutual friend had subscribed to the setup principle known as "He's Jewish; therefore he's perfect for you." This was, of course, only a slight variation of the "pulse and penis" principle that I'd run into in Bend. And it caused me considerable concern. Now the people who actually *knew* me thought I was desperate?

Apparently so, as "He's Jewish/he's perfect" seemed to be the guiding principle behind most of my fix-ups over the next several months. These included dates with (1) a twenty-six-year-old peace activist whose first question was, "So, did you have good sex with your last boyfriend?" (2) a mathematics graduate student who professed a deep-seated paranoia about health clubs, and (3) a graphic designer with whom, it turned out, I'd been set up ten years earlier. All I remembered about our painful first date was that I'd excused myself before dessert by telling him I had to go watch *thirtysomething*—appalling behavior that I would have felt more guilty about had it not been my favorite program that season.

By the time the first of my two cousins' weddings rolled around, about ten months after I'd returned, I hadn't gotten beyond a second date, let alone found someone I'd want to invite to a marriage ceremony. I had to admit I was getting a little impatient, but not as much as my grandparents were. During the break between the wedding ceremony and the party, Grandma Honey cornered me in the restroom and snapped, "You need to find a man—a professional man," at which point she turned on her heel and bolted out the door. I'd once read in a magazine that you could successfully fight tears by smiling repeatedly, and that night, after standing at the sink for a good ten minutes, I found out it worked.

Barely two months after that, I showed up dateless at my other cousin's wedding. Fortunately, I was seated next to Jen and John, so at least I didn't have to endure the usual Singles Table trauma. Even better, Grandma Honey was seated on the opposite side of the ballroom, and I didn't run into her the entire evening. However, the reception did have its awkward moments, like when Jen and John got up to dance and I was left alone to munch on the chocolate candy that was the only edible food at this vegan affair.

My first year back in L.A. was coming to an end, and I was no closer to finding love than I'd been in Bend. Other than BikeMan, the only person who'd seen me undressed was my gynecologist, who had the irritating habit of asking, "So, are you sexually active?" I wanted to reply, "Are you?"

I thought back to those last days in Oregon when I was walking on air, and I remembered what had made me feel that way besides all those sexy e-mails. I'd had hope—real, tangible hope. Now, a year later, I was wondering if I'd ever feel that way again.

Day 1400
B.C.E.

Day 1
C.E.

Day 1000
C.E.

14

Singled Out

$\mathcal{T}$here are many transitions to be endured once you've crossed the Great Divide between under-thirty and over-thirty singleness, but none are more dreaded than the move from "single" to "still single." You know how it goes. In your twenties, people ask "Is she single?" with the cheery hopefulness that they can set you up with their darling cousin who just moved up from San Diego. But at some undefined point in your early thirties, the Dr. Jekyll question turns into the Miss Hyde "Is she *still* single?"—spoken with the same tone reserved for questions like, "Is it herpes?"

Just when your lack of marital status has turned into some sort of disease, the remedy becomes even more scarce. No longer can you assume that any cute guy you might bump into—at a coffee bar, in line at the movies—is single. The only clue to help you deduce his eligibility is the presence of a wedding band, so you develop a habit of making a visual beeline from a guy's face to the ring finger on his left hand. Still, there are occasions when this screening process doesn't work. For instance: What if the guy is wearing weight-lifting gloves?

That's the situation I was up against with a redheaded guy I spotted at my health club. He wasn't tall or classically handsome, but he had broad shoulders and an unmistakable down-to-earth quality. Although he must have been quite muscular, judging from the heavy barbells he could lift, he wasn't one to show off his body, preferring to wear baggy T-shirts. And then there were those gloves, which he always wore. But even though I couldn't tell if he was married, one thing was obvious: I was feeling a spark. Despite knowing absolutely nothing about the guy, I was magnetically drawn. It was like he was the anti-BikeMan.

One night when we coincidentally convened at the triceps-dip machine, I struck up a conversation and he seemed receptive. I mentioned that I'd recently moved from Oregon, and he asked what city I'd lived in and what I'd been doing there. I asked about his job, and he said he was a lawyer with the Securities and Exchange Commission. What luck! Not only was he friendly and inquisitive, but he was smart, too!

The next time, I got his name: Adam. In an effort to determine whether he was single, I presented the evidence—his friendliness, the long hours he spent in the gym, the fact that he'd never mentioned a wife or girlfriend—to several of my friends. But their analysis was inconclusive. A married guy wouldn't necessarily mention his wife right off because he might enjoy the attention, noted one of my married guy friends.

I kept running into Adam, and we'd chat. He did not seem to be dismissing me—I knew that tone of voice well, and he never used it. Maybe he was just shy. Next time, I vowed to take the initiative.

But before I had a chance, he disappeared. No matter what day or time I worked out, he was nowhere to be found. After a few weeks, I became distressed because I had just bought a condo on the other side of town and would soon be joining a different gym. Where had Adam gone? How could I find him? What if he was the One and I had blown my big chance? I knew I couldn't get any personal information about him from the gym without a subpoena.

But then I came up with a plan that—perhaps I should say for the sake of full disclosure—no member of my cabinet endorsed. I didn't know Adam's last name; but I did know, assuming he was telling the truth, that he worked for the SEC somewhere in Los Angeles. Guessing that his office was near the gym, I used the telephone directory to track down the closest SEC location. Then I wrote a note that began, "Dear Adam, Don't worry—I'm not a stalker!" (But come to think of it, wasn't I?) I explained the reasons for my unorthodox approach—his disappearance from the gym, my imminent move across town—and gave him my number in case he was single and interested in meeting for coffee. "If not," I wrote, "just toss this note and be flattered!"

I addressed the letter to the Securities and Exchange Commission "c/o Adam, Attorney with Red Hair." Then, for nearly ten minutes, I stood before my corner mailbox, the envelope dangling from my fingertips. Finally, I dropped it in.

Three days later, I came home to the following phone message: "Hi, Suzanne. This is Adam, the redheaded attorney with the SEC. Got your note. I'm very flattered, but I'm married, so I can't take you up on your offer. But that was a really ballsy thing to do. Good luck with your move!"

Despite the blow—which, of course, was cushioned by

the fact I knew I was playing a long shot—I did take some comfort in the thoughtfulness of his message. He was indeed the nice guy I'd pegged him to be. Still, I was starting to develop a bit of anxiety over what kind of person I was turning into. Writing to strangers was just part of it. Then there was the purchase of my condo.

Yes, I was doing it for all the practical reasons. Now that I was committed to staying in L.A., it didn't make sense to keep paying my hefty rent when I could own a place for practically the same monthly outlay. No less than Alan Greenspan would have advised me to buy that condo. Plus, I did adore the place, with its hardwood floors, thick crown moldings, and sturdy 1940s construction. And I knew that, with my sister's decorating help and the removal of the wall-to-wall bedroom mirrors that looked like something out of a porn movie, the condo was going to be smashing.

And yet, I couldn't help feeling as if I'd missed a step. The natural progression is supposed to be single-married-mortgage, right? It wasn't that I'd harbored fantasies of being carried over the threshold of my first home by Mr. Right, but it did feel a little lonely walking through the front door with two guys from Wetzel and Sons moving company.

There was no shortage of people willing to comment on the fact that I was defying the natural progression. At the gym, a guy I occasionally worked out with had this to say when I told him I'd closed escrow: "You've already given up on finding a husband?"

My grandparents seemed to think so. They made a generous contribution to my down payment—the same amount that they had given my cousin to help cover the cost of her wedding. "We probably won't live to see you married," Grandma Honey said, "so you might as well put it to good use now."

Even the state of California seemed obsessed with pointing out my single state, requiring me to sign several legal documents that defined me as a SINGLE WOMAN (NEVER MARRIED) True, this was for my own protection; if I ever divorced, my ex would not be able to claim half the property, by virtue of the fact that I was a SINGLE WOMAN (NEVER MARRIED) at the time of the purchase. Still, I could have lived without the reminder. And the very idea of a former husband seemed especially ludicrous considering I had yet to locate a future one.

Okay, so maybe I shouldn't have taken my escrow documents so personally. But I did have to wonder: Was my real estate purchase the first step down the slippery slope to becoming a frumpy gray-haired lady in elastic pants who spends her retirement years roaming the country in a Winnebago?

That image alone sent me diving back into match.com.

This time, I was determined to get it right. From BikeMan, I knew the hazards of too much e-mail, and my most recent history had shown me the disastrous results of choosing guys practically at random. A more scientific method seemed in order. And so, modeling myself after the FBI profilers who specialize in identifying serial killers, I sought to devise my own diagnostic techniques for pinpointing probable boyfriends.

I began to study the essays more carefully, analyzing the language to detect that elusive combination of genuineness, good humor, and intelligence. My methodology narrowed the possibilities down to a select few. It also ferreted out a previously unrecognized category of instant rejects: the Equally Comfortable Guy.

These were men—and I found a surprising number of

them—who professed to want a woman who was "equally comfortable riding in a limo to a black-tie affair as she is watching TV while having a beer." Or, alternately phrased, "a lady who's equally comfortable at the Ritz or the pool hall." Or, as yet another guy put it: "a girl who is equally comfortable going camping as she is dressing in a sexy black evening gown."

I couldn't figure out why these guys were demanding equal comfort levels with events that normally take place with radically unequal frequency. What kind of people ride in limos as often as they watch TV? I also couldn't imagine the woman who read this description and said, "How uncanny! That's me! I just love looking drop-dead gorgeous at formal affairs as much as tossing back a few cold ones with the guys over a game of eight ball!" But, come to think of it, maybe that's every guy's absurd fantasy.

Fortunately, there were plenty of match.com guys who seemed to have more realistic expectations, and with my improved decoding skills, I was able to identify several promising prospects. The next step was to initiate an e-mail correspondence to test the waters. If, after three or four days of exchanges, I sensed a face-to-face meeting was in order, I suggested a Starbucks summit. (The meeting was almost always at my instigation. For reasons that escape me, most guys seemed to want to e-mail indefinitely.)

My friend Margie, who was also single and dabbling in match.com, came up with a handy measurement system that helped me gauge my level of interest: How much of my charm was I turning on to make an impression with the guy?

"So the psychologist you went out with—what percentage?" Margie would call to ask after I'd gotten home from one of my predates.

Early on, my date selections were so off base that I didn't bother to put forth more than a ten- to twenty-percent effort. In the case of a lawyer who couldn't seem to remember my occupation—"So, wait, you're some kind of writer?" he asked three times during our thirty-minute coffee date—I'd actually expended zero percent. But now I was meeting guys whom I at least enjoyed talking to, and I was routinely in the fifty- to seventy-five-percent range. Still, no sparks. Or even second dates. The handful of guys who did ask me out again were inevitably the ones whom I'd dismissed for lack of chemistry. And the few times I tried to initiate a second date, that same lack-of-chemistry line came right back at me.

One benefit of my improved screening skills was that I was spending less time logged on to match.com. I'd check in once or a twice a day to see if any good prospects had joined the service, and I was averaging one coffee date a week, but I wasn't consumed by the process and had plenty of time to go about all my usual routines.

Meanwhile, the Schlosberg family social calendar was in full throttle, and as usual, I was showing up dateless to every family event. At our annual celebration of the Jewish New Year, the evening progressed predictably enough. The dinner conversation was dominated by a debate over whether brisket should be cooked for six hours at 275 degrees or for four hours at 325 degrees. After dessert was served, Jen and John clinked their wineglasses with spoons and stood up from the table.

I glanced up from my noodle kugel but didn't stop eating, figuring they were about to kick off the expected series of toasts, which are generally some version of the Schlosberg Family Event Multipurpose Speech. This speech—varying in length from thirty seconds (me) to ten minutes (my mother) to twenty-five minutes (Grandma Honey)—typically involves praising our family for being the best, most loving, most generous, most adept-at-cooking-brisket family that ever graced this earth. There are more toasts offered at any given Schlosberg family event than there are, I imagine, at any White House function involving visiting heads of state. In fact, failure to give a speech is considered a serious affront. At Grandma Honey's eighty-eighth birthday dinner, for example, Grandpa Julius stood up, pointed at my cousin's husband of five months, and roared, "Kevin, we haven't heard from you yet!"

But as it turned out, Jen and John's toast wasn't a toast at all. "We have an announcement to make!" John began, beaming. The two of them looked each other, then shouted in unison, "We're engaged!"

Remember what happened after the Berlin Wall came down? Well, that is about the only other event in recent history to have generated the sort of shrieking, hugging, crying, and sustained euphoria that took place in my parents' dining room at that very moment. I'm sure I must have shrieked right along with the rest of them, but it wasn't out of pure, unadulterated happiness for the joyful couple.

Don't get me wrong. I was thrilled that my sister had found such a gem, and I considered John the best potential brother-in-law a girl could ask for, especially now that he no longer looked like Mike Myers in *Wayne's World*, having allowed Angela to chop a good ten inches off his hair.

But remarkably, Jen's engagement caught me by complete surprise. Yes, yes . . . I know I should have seen it coming. John had moved into Jen's apartment, and he had long since become a member of our family, assuming the role of Grandpa's restroom chaperone at events where the facilities required more than a twenty-foot walk. But just like all those poor people who chose to remain on Mount St. Helens as it was about to blow, I'd brushed off all the warning signs. On top of that, Jen and John had not thought to alert me to their plans, even though they had regularly commiserated with me about my state of singleness. Surely they could have foreseen the emotional equivalent of a billion tons of ash and molten lava that would be hurtling in my direction.

It arrived even before the hugging and crying had subsided. I'd already heard more than enough comments during the engagements and weddings of my two younger cousins. But now, with my younger sister beating me to the altar, it was just like the mortgage: A step had been skipped. Once again, the natural order of things was being defied.

"*You* should be the one getting engaged!" Grandma Ruth exclaimed loud enough for the next suburb to hear. "When are *you* going to find a man?"

"Well, at least now there's hope for Carl and Judy to have grandkids!" shouted a family friend who was sitting right next to me.

The gloves had come off. To everyone in the room, I wasn't just the maid of honor. I was the old maid of honor.

I saw the next few months laid out in vivid and garish detail: the flurry of showers and parties; the endless discussions of wedding registries, floral themes, and guest lists; the buzz of anticipation and excitement. The only topic of conversation in my family—in fact, the very reason for existence—would be my sister's wedding. And I would be the murmured backstory. I could already hear my parents: "Yes, Jennifer is our daughter who's getting married. Suzanne . . . no, she's *still single*."

My only hope was that it would be a short engagement. But Jen and John had other ideas. They disclosed that they didn't plan to get married for sixteen months because my sister wanted to get her new graphic design business off the ground before being consumed by the minutiae of wedding planning. My parents begged Jen and John to move the date up. Not for my sake, of course. They were afraid my grandparents might not live long enough to see the big day.

Personally, I had no doubt that my grandparents, despite countless physical ailments, could will themselves to stay alive until the wedding, as the event offered them unprecedented opportunities. Grandma Honey, for one, could make one of her trademark rambling speeches in front of her biggest audience ever, and no one would dare organize a filibuster, as we've sometimes done when she gets carried away at small family gatherings. Grandpa Julius would be given a free pass to hurl insults at the valet parking attendants, bartenders, busboys, and servers ("You don't know your ass from your elbow!" is a favorite) because everyone would be too preoccupied to tell him to shut up. Grandma Ruth, meanwhile, would have me trapped for hours on end, enabling her to torment me in public about the dreadfulness of being over thirty and single. The way I saw it, my grandparents had plenty to live for. Their survival was never in doubt.

Ultimately, Jen and John won their case, and I realized there was a bright side. At least I would be awarded additional time to find a companion for the wedding. Of course, a mere date would not suffice for an event laden with such implications. If I showed up with some stranger, it would be obvious that he was just window dressing. What I needed was a bona fide boyfriend, someone who would at least offer the suggestion of a genuine prospect. Besides that, I knew I'd need the moral support. It was a tall order, to be sure.

Though the wedding preparations wouldn't reach a fevered pitch for months, I was treated to a preview of things to come shortly after the announcement, when some friends invited my parents, Jen and John, and me to the Beverly Hills Hotel for dinner. After toasting the engaged couple, the hostess looked over at me and added, "And congratulations to Suzanne on her new condominium purchase!" It couldn't have been more clear if it had been pasted on a billboard: Jen had a marriage. I had a mortgage. I shuddered to think what praise would have been heaped on me had I not recently become a member of a condo owners' association. "Congratulations to Suzanne on her new fax machine!"

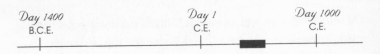

Day 1400
B.C.E.

Day 1
C.E.

Day 1000
C.E.

15

Going Bust in Jackpot

*A*s the countdown for Jen and John's wedding began, another deadline was coming up even faster. Just two months away was the biggest couples' event in modern history: New Year's Eve 1999. Now the entire retail world was selling a barrage of opportunities for conspicuous romantic consumption. Hotels, restaurants, clubs, airlines, resorts, champagne makers—they all were vying to be every couple's choice to usher in the New Millennium.

Between my family's hysteria over the engagement and the planet's hysteria over the coming of 2000, my first impulse was to book a room on the International Space Station. I scanned the United Airlines Web site to see how far my stash of frequent-flyer miles could take me and decided that Tonga sounded like a sufficiently remote destination. I knew nothing about the island other than the fact that its four hundred-pound king was on a mission to solve his nation's obesity problem, offering residents free toasters and sneakers as a reward for losing weight. On *60*

Minutes I'd seen the monarch himself taking a power walk. Surely there would be a StairMaster for me in Tonga.

I perked up when the United representative said I could fly there by December 31, but then he discovered there were no available return tickets until March. Being stranded in the South Pacific for three months didn't sound like such a bad deal. On the other hand, it would put me seriously behind on my work assignments, not to mention my search for a guy. From what I'd seen on *60 Minutes,* I was not likely to find a match in Tonga.

Deep down, I knew Tonga was just an extreme reaction to my impulse to flee. In reality, I didn't have to go all the way to the South Pacific to escape all the coupled-up revelry in L.A. I turned to the Internet for more practical New Year's Eve ideas and decided that a concert might work. I'd blend into the crowd, and the entertainment would distract me. While browsing a country-music site, I came upon the perfect event: a Joe Diffie concert in Jackpot, Nevada.

Joe Diffie is an affable, blond country singer with a bushy mustache, a mullet haircut, and a stable of upbeat, generic tunes about jukeboxes, ex-wives, and pickup trucks. I had never considered buying one of Joe Diffie's albums or seeing him in concert, and I can tell you that if Joe Diffie had been playing in my neighborhood on New Year's Eve—or any night, really—I wouldn't have made the effort.

I felt even less of an affinity for Jackpot, a tiny desert gambling town just south of the Idaho border. I had been to Jackpot once, in high school, on the way back from an Idaho ski trip after our rented motorhome had spun out on the highway ice and crashed into an embankment just outside of town. I had never planned on making a return visit.

But there was something strangely appealing about driving 750 miles to see a second-rate country singer in a fourth-rate gambling town on the eve of the New Millennium. It would be my personal protest against all the hype and hoopla. Everyone else was vying to come up with the greatest, most sensational, most dramatic way to ring in the New Year. I figured, Why not do just the opposite? What could be less spectacular and exotic than driving up U.S. 93 to see Joe Diffie play Cactus Pete's Casino? Besides, this plan would fulfill my desire to split town without being gone too long or spending too much money. I could do the entire 1,500-mile round trip in three days and stay at a Motel 6. I was set! I had a plan for the New Millennium!

When I called Cactus Pete's to make a reservation, the customer service agent asked, "Do you want two tickets or four?" Now, I've never been the type to shrink from doing things alone or admitting that I had, but there was something about the Mother of All New Year's Eves that put me on the defensive. Too self-conscious to say, "Just one, please," I took the pair. Anyway, I rationalized, maybe a miracle would occur, and I would meet a guy who was willing to come along. And in the more likely case that I had to absorb the cost of the second ticket, well, it was still a lot cheaper than a three-month hotel stay in Tonga.

Naturally, I did not mention my plan to my parents. They would have disapproved for more reasons than I cared to count. Instead, I told them I was going on a road trip to visit friends in Reno and Salt Lake City, offering them an itinerary too vague for them to track me down.

When I told my plan to Nancy, she was predictably appalled. "Couldn't you just do something normal, like stay home and watch TV?"

But, I pointed out, that's exactly what I'd done for my New Year's Eve in Bend, and the next day I'd ended up making the four-hundred-mile drive to Winnemucca, yet another desolate Nevada gambling town.

"See? It makes perfect sense," I explained to Nancy. "I'm just cutting to the chase."

Two months passed, along with another dozen futile Starbucks predates; and not surprisingly, no suitable male surfaced to accompany me to Jackpot. So I stocked the Trooper with Twizzlers, candy corns, and CDs and headed north, grateful that I was fleeing the happy couples who would be partying in L.A.

I spent the first night in Caliente, Nevada (population 200), which I added to my list of "Twilight Zone" towns à la Alturas, California, the place with the rotary telephones. When the Caliente motel clerk asked for a photo ID, I explained that I'd recently surrendered my Oregon driver's license and my temporary California license didn't have a picture. "But I do have my passport!" I offered. (In L.A., I'd been pestered so often for a photo ID that I'd begun to carry it around.) The clerk appeared baffled by the term "passport" and said, "Just forget about it, okay?"

I arrived the next evening in Jackpot, a lone cluster of bright lights shining in the desert darkness. It was about 7:30 P.M., nearly showtime. At the Cactus Pete's box office, I learned that I'd lucked out: My reservation had been lost, so I only had to pay for one ticket. There were still plenty of seats available, proving that I had succeeded in choosing one of the world's least-popular ways to celebrate the coming of the New Millennium.

The concert venue was intimate, with a capacity of maybe 150, and I was seated at a table for eight only a few feet from the stage. I thought I'd timed it just right to avoid small talk with my table companions before the music began, but the band was getting a late start. As I took my seat, the others at the table were making their introductions. The fortyish woman to my right, with big blond hair and bright red nails, said her name was Heidi and introduced her mother, Willie, a hefty seventyish woman with a gray beehive hairdo and a thick German accent. Heidi and Willie said they were from the San Francisco Bay area, and I mentioned I'd lived there before moving to Oregon and then Los Angeles. I could see the look of confusion in their eyes when they suddenly realized I was the only person at our table who had come to the concert alone. "Vaht are you doink here by yourself?" Willie demanded to know.

The truth was way too embarrassing, so I scrambled to come up with a plausible story. "Oh, well, there's not much to tell," I said. "My boyfriend—I mean, my ex-boyfriend— and I are huge Joe Diffie fans, and we bought our tickets months ago. But then, last Thursday we broke up"—I threw in a sigh to suggest it was too painful to talk about— "and just to prove to myself I didn't need him, I decided to come here anyway." I mustered a brave smile.

All in all, I thought, a good lie, one that surely would keep them from prying. I was wrong.

"Vhy did you break up?" Willie immediately responded.

"Was it a fight?" Heidi added. "Was he cheating on you?"

Forced to think on my feet, I used as many details as I could from my past. I figured it would be easiest to keep my story straight if my "boyfriend" was a cop named Alec. But my house of cards began to collapse when Willie asked me which law enforcement agency Alec worked for. Instinctively

I said "Berkeley PD," to which she replied, "But didn't you say you lived in L.A. and Oregon before zat?"

Not only was I getting confused by my own story, but I also was getting testy. Now I was having to justify my singleness to strangers at a Nevada casino?

Fortunately, the band rescued me before I had made a complete idiot of myself. Diffie put on a pleasantly diverting concert, and once the lights came up, I attempted to make a quick escape. But Heidi and Willie would have none of it. "Suzanne, vee must do sahmsing about your boyfriend," Willie announced. "Vee must make him jealous!"

She looked at my camera and then glanced over to the band members, who were now packing up their instruments, and before I knew it, she had run onto the stage and flagged down the bass player.

"Zis girl vas jilted by her boyfriend," I heard her say as she pointed vigorously toward me. "She needs a photograph vis you to make him jealous!"

I valiantly tried to wave them off, but Willie ignored me.

"Suzanne, come! Come!" she commanded with an authority that also seemed to be holding the bass player in place.

Even after I had joined her onstage and pointed out to her the bass player's wedding band, she refused to be deterred. Heidi commandeered my camera, and Willie blocked the scene like a Hollywood director.

"Come closer!" she instructed the bass player. "Remember zat you sink she is sexy!"

A couples' party in L.A. was suddenly not sounding so bad.

After the show, I surrendered to the force of Willie and accompanied her and Heidi to the casino's dinner buffet.

Willie reiterated my saga to the poor waiter, who didn't seem to understand a word she was saying through her thick accent. He also appeared completely baffled as to why I was posing for a photo with my arms around his shoulders and Willie's "New Year's Eve 2000" crown on his head. During dinner, Heidi and Willie continued to interrogate me about my breakup, but this time I managed to steer the conversation toward country music. It turned out that Willie and Heidi were die-hard fans.

"Last time we saw Joe Diffie, I got the phone number of his drummer!" Heidi bragged.

"Villie Nelson really turns me up," Willie offered. I assumed she meant "turns me on," but I didn't really want clarification.

The moment we finished eating, I said my good-byes, fearful they might rope me into a photo with one of the security guards. Besides, I had a good excuse to cut out: I still had to drive an hour to my motel. The three Jackpot motels had been booked, so I was staying down the highway in Wells. When the New Millennium dawned, I was somewhere on U.S. 93, feeling an immense sense of relief. I'd survived New Year's Eve, and the worst that had happened was that I'd had to fabricate an ex-boyfriend.

Now I was ready to come home and face the task at hand: I had a little less than fourteen months to find a real boyfriend. As I headed back across the desert, I realized it had been well over a year since I'd had sex, and I wondered why my task was proving to be so difficult—why, after dozens of dates, I had come up empty while most of my friends and relatives were pairing off. It occurred to me that maybe the problem wasn't with the guys out there. Maybe it was me.

Day 1400
B.C.E.

Day 1
C.E.

Day 1000
C.E.

16

~~~~~~~~~~~~~~~~~~~~~~~~~~~~~

Am I Hot or Not?

*A*t what point does any garden-variety predicament esca-
late to the level of full-blown crisis? At what moment does
a food shortage become a famine? At what instant does a
recession become a depression? When does a little sexual
indiscretion become Monica-gate?

That's what happened to me with the Streak: At some
point in the mid five hundreds I realized that I'd crossed
some invisible line, and it was time to assign my crisis a
name and keep track of it with a number.

Coming up with the name, the Streak, was easy. So was
the initial calculation. The last time I'd had sex, my final
romp with BikeMan, was exactly three weeks after I'd
returned home from Bend, and the move date was etched in
my consciousness as well as my day planner. But, you may
ask, why bother even doing the math?

All right, I'll admit it. Quantifying your misery does
help you get more mileage out of it. I mean, does anyone

really care if some human-rights activist hasn't eaten for a while? Ah, but when he's on a "twenty-seven-day hunger strike," well, that's really saying something. Does anyone pay attention if Texas is having a heat wave? But if it's "day forty-two of 100-plus temperatures"—well, there's a bona fide media event!

Not that I've ever intended to issue any press releases about the Streak, but I do think that the sheer magnitude of the number has helped my friends understand the gravity of my situation. Every so often someone says, "Oh, Suzanne, it can't be *that* bad! I once went a whole year without sex!" To which I can reply: "Oh, *really*?" Then I can quantify my distress down to the particular number of days.

Usually, the statistics leave them speechless.

Now don't get the wrong idea: My streak isn't something I've tallied on a daily basis, like Ted Koppel during the Iran Hostage Crisis. But every time I've hit a day of significance, like New Year's Eve or Valentine's Day or my birthday, I have instinctively done a recalculation. If anything, I figure it will somehow boost the odds that I will, eventually, break it. All crises end at some point, don't they? It may have taken 444 days, but the Iran hostages finally did come home. Surely, at some point, my own crisis will come to a dramatic—no, a climactic!—conclusion.

Not all my friends have been convinced by my logic. "Are you sure you should even be calling it a streak?" one friend said. "I mean, when something goes on that long, isn't it more accurately called a 'lifestyle'?"

Of course, she was only joking, but I wasn't laughing that hard. "Oh, you know that's not what I meant," she said, backtracking. "Even lifestyles can be temporary. Most hippies didn't stay hippies forever, right?"

For several months after I started counting, I used the Streak whenever I was in need of a little sympathy, and the strategy worked. The number did make an impression on people, eliciting both shock and condolences. But then as it entered high triple digits, the Streak began to backfire. Sentiment started to shift from "Gee, that's really awful" to "Gee, Suzanne, what's your problem?"

Now, it's not as if I had never considered that the Streak might be of my own making. The statistics alone suggested something more was at play than just bad luck. By the time New Year's 2000 rolled around, I had screened thousands of potential boyfriends on match.com, and of these, I had corresponded with at least three hundred. Eliminating men who sent e-mails like "My best friend is my hairless little dog" and "I can spot a Degas at twenty paces—can you?" I had met for coffee with about forty. Yet I had only made it past a first date once, with an architect named Joe, who treated his fork and plate as a percussion instrument. (More on that later.)

If a baseball player struck out thirty-nine times in forty at-bats, wouldn't that suggest a flaw in his swing?

Clearly, something was amiss. Yet for the longest time I'd resisted the idea that the problem was with me. Obviously, it was much easier—not to mention much less confidence shattering—to blame my predicament on the rest of the world. But when my friends began subtly suggesting that I take a look in the mirror, I could no longer avoid the issue. Over time, their comments were becoming more pointed ("I'm sure you don't want to hear this, but . . ."), and I realized that factions were forming around full-blown theories.

So after Jackpot, I swallowed hard and came around to the idea of self-examination. If the problem did turn out to

be me, I figured, I'd actually have new reason to hope.
Surely it would be easier to change myself than the rest of
the world.

By far the most popular theory at the time was, in
the words of Grandma Ruth, "You're too picky." It was
alternately known as "You're too critical," "You're not
open-minded," and "Who do you think you are, Gwyneth
Paltrow?"

This theory had picked up steam after I attempted to
institute a new, more discriminating policy governing
setups. Weary from so many failed blind dates, I told my
friends they would now have to articulate three sound reasons why their great guy and I might hit it off—not counting single, Jewish, and "he has a condo on the Westside."
When apprised of the new rules, most people were bewil-
dered, as if I'd just asked them to name three reasons why
the European Union should accept Poland. "Hmmm, let me
think about it and get back to you," they'd say before permanently dropping the subject.

Some told me flat-out that I was being shortsighted and
unappreciative, as if I were a homeless person refusing the
offer of a warm bed unless the sheets were 300 thread
count. In this camp was Sheila, a family friend who called
to set me up with a Jewish Westside condo owner. After she
summarily dismissed my "three sound reasons" rule, our
conversation went as follows:

Me: So what's he like?
Sheila: Well, I know he's a successful stockbroker!
Me: So you haven't actually met him?
Sheila: Well, I know both of his parents, and they are
        very good people.

Me: Is he athletic?

Sheila: Well, he must be—he's six feet tall.

Me: Is there *anything* you know about this guy?

Sheila: Well, I know for a *fact* that he's looking to get married.

I told Sheila I appreciated the thought but that—having already expended the time and energy on dead-end blind dates that I could have spent mastering golf or conversational French—I needed better reasons to fight for a parking spot at Starbucks. She snapped back, "Well, forget it, then. There are plenty of women in his office who are interested in him."

Although I felt justified turning down Sheila's offer, I did wonder if I was setting my sights too high. Was I, in fact, being too picky? Maybe there was no such thing as the Perfect Guy. Or maybe he was living in Perth, Australia, and we would never meet. Perhaps I really was expecting too much.

"You know, you can't just reject every guy who doesn't live for *Law & Order,*" Nancy said.

But that had never been the case. I didn't have a checklist of trivial requirements. Unlike some women I knew, I wasn't disqualifying men because they didn't make a certain amount of money or didn't have a graduate degree. And I certainly wasn't as obnoxiously nitpicky as some of the men I'd run across on match.com, like CheckMeOut, a self-described "venture capitalist" who wrote, "Seeking a gorgeous, exotic woman who is my intellectual equal. No offense, but please do not reply if you weigh more than 130 lbs."

When I dismissed a prospect, I did so with the certitude that any reasonable woman in my position would have done the same. Yes, I will confess that I did reject a few guys on the basis of looks alone, but only if they flunked the Newt Gingrich Test: Would I rather have sex with this guy or Newt Gingrich? But far more typically, the reason was because they were arrogant ("It stuns me that I'm still single," one lawyer told me) or had the personality of a toolbox. Or because they would have grated on anybody's nerves.

In deference to the "too picky" theory, I did make some minor adjustments to my search process. In the "what I'm looking for" section on match.com, I loosened my age, height, and geographical ranges. But ultimately, I decided there was a definite line between "not ready to settle" and "too choosy," and I had not crossed it. Yet.

While the "You're too picky" theory reigned, its corollary—"You're too quick to judge"—had also gained favor among some friends. According to this hypothesis, my mistake wasn't that I was dismissing guys for the wrong reasons but that I was dismissing them too quickly. "Maybe the guys you assume are boring are really just shy," Nancy offered. "Maybe the ones who talk about themselves obsessively are just nervous. Did you ever think of that? Could you maybe go on a date that lasts longer than the seventh-inning stretch?"

Okay, it was true that I had been making snap judgments. Most of my predates lasted well under an hour. The shortest one, twelve minutes with a fiction writer named Tim, began like this:

"I seriously hope that's not what you're eating for dinner," Tim said after I ordered a piece of cake and a grande espresso Frappuccino at Starbucks. His snide tone told me he wasn't joking.

"No," I replied, instantly ratcheting down my charm by about sixty percentage points, "but since I had to rush to meet you after my *eighty-mile bike ride,* I didn't have time to eat. I thought this might tide me over."

Tim railed on about the overpriced coffee drinks, the hostile nature of match.com women, and the idiocy of people who watch TV. I extricated myself with the first excuse that popped into my head. "I'm so sorry," I said, glancing at my watch as I got up from the table, "but the milk in my fridge just expired, and I've got to get to the supermarket."

Of course, not all the guys I went out with were so easy to judge in an instant. But I did feel that my profiler skills were serving me pretty well. Ann, my secretary of uncommon wisdom, disapproved of my approach and offered what seemed to be an important insight.

"What you're not grasping," she said, "is that there are degrees of sparkness." Ann counseled me not to expect instant combustion. Some sparks take time to appear, and some need even more time to ignite. She also warned me not to wait around for the Big Spark, as it can come with its own hazards. "The biggest Big Spark relationship I ever had ended when the Spark Guy threatened to put my head through a wall," she said, adding that she ran screaming out of her house and called the police.

I kept Ann's advice in mind during a coffee date with Joe, an architect from Wyoming. I didn't feel any particular connection with him, perhaps because of his strange habit of looking in every direction—to my left, to my right, over my head—but mine. Still, he was handsome and seemed easygoing, a good test subject for the degrees-of-sparkness premise. I decided to give him the benefit of the doubt and attribute his lack of eye contact to anxiety.

In fact, I was so eager to test out Ann's premise that I asked him out—via e-mail, the most risk-free approach—

the day after our coffee date, and he readily agreed. (We'd ended the date with a hug and the not-atypical, "Well, talk to you online!" When you're enmeshed in the world of Internet dating, it's easy to forget about the invention known as the telephone.)

For the second date, Joe and I met up at a Cuban restaurant, where he ended up eating an entire half a garlic chicken while looking directly at the couple seated next to us. I was tempted to pull up a chair at their table just to see if I could get Joe to look at me. I still felt no spark, but he still hadn't done anything egregious. So with Ann's comments in mind, I used e-mail to initiate a third date. Again Joe seemed game, and this time we went to an Indian restaurant, where he spent the evening looking directly at the elderly couple next to us while pumping me for ideas on how to improve his match.com profile. He also caused a racket, stabbing every grain of rice on his tin plate until it was clean. When he dropped me off at my condo, I barely waited for his car to come to a complete stop before I jumped out.

My experience with Joe was only Exhibit A in my defense, but I decided it was enough. The "too hasty" theory was out. I really could trust my first impressions.

Still, there was no shortage of backup theories to explain my singlehood.

My single friend Melanie suggested I was too aggressive and should stop asking guys out. "It's unfortunate, but you've got to let guys take the initiative," she said. "It's a weakness in the male animal, but everything has got to be their idea. It's like a biological imperative." I couldn't believe that one of my very own friends was subscribing to *The Rules*. Was I also supposed to wait two days to return a guy's calls and never talk to him on the phone for more than ten minutes?

I dismissed Melanie's theory pretty quickly because (1) she was thirty-nine and never married—where had this strategy gotten *her*?, and (2) my male friends thought it was ridiculous. I got a persuasive rebuttal from Allan, a married jeweler I'd recently gotten to know through cycling. He'd quickly been promoted to cabinet level due to his insight into all things male and the fact that, as a freelancer who worked at home, he had lots of time on his hands to discuss these issues.

"If a guy is interested," countered my advisor on male affairs, "he's not going to be turned off just because a woman asked him out. Actually it's the opposite: He's going to be flattered." Allan said that guys don't mind taking the initiative—it's what they're bred to do, and they're used to being rejected—but they find it refreshing when a woman relieves them of the responsibility. I'd figured as much. After all, Alec had responded to "Are you interested in me or *not*?" with a smile and a kiss.

Another camp argued that my big mistake was the very act of searching for a boyfriend. "Just live your life and it'll happen when you least expect it," said Dana, the eternal optimist.

I'd actually tried this theory on for size—partly out of a conscious effort but mostly because of blind-date fatigue. Twice I'd abandoned Internet dating for a couple months at a time and had just gone about my life. However, since my life consisted of bicycling at 6:30 A.M. with a club made up primarily of married guys, doing phone interviews with exercise physiologists from my home office, and watching *Law & Order* reruns, the chances of randomly meeting any guy, let alone the right guy, were slim. It was against my nature to sit back and do nothing, so every time I quit match.com, I inevitably signed back up (at a higher monthly rate, naturally).

Dana offered up another theory, applauding me for trying so hard but suggesting I was looking for love in all the wrong places. "You've *got* to take up rock-climbing," she insisted. "The sport is like ninety-five percent male." (In her valiant attempt to be helpful, Dana subscribed to all of the major theories at one point or another, even though several of them contradicted each other.)

A guy friend recommended I buy a Harley-Davidson motorcycle, arguing that "Harley guys like strong women." I thought that was the dumbest idea I'd heard until my friend Cristina, the Bend artist, outdid herself with this outrageous idea: "Go hang out at the dump! A woman can really get a lot of attention there! Whenever I go unload my old canvases, guys are always fighting to help."

What all of these friends seemed to be missing was that I had no interest in any of these activities. (Loitering at the *dump*?) If I wanted to find someone compatible, it seemed I should be looking for someone whose hobbies appealed to me. Considering I was deathly afraid of motorcycles, did I really want to try to become a biker babe?

Though I never put much stock in the "looking in the wrong places" theory, at least these friends were coming up with concrete suggestions. Which is more than I can say for the "get therapy" theorists. These were the friends who kept insisting that if only I would see a shrink, I would begin to give off the sort of vibes that would draw men to me like mosquitoes to a bug zapper. Kate, who had spent most of her adulthood in therapy, was the one who pushed the hardest.

"What you need to do is get rid of your emotional bag-gage," she said, swearing that the therapy after her failed first marriage had magically attracted the great love of her life. "Once you deal with your issues, you'll find that a rela-tionship will just 'happen.'"

But I knew exactly what my issues were: I hadn't had sex in two years and it sucked. Notably, none of the Therapy Theorists had ever experienced singlehood after age thirty. They also didn't seem to grasp that, even with-out a boyfriend and despite all my kvetching, I considered myself essentially a happy person. I'd made a fine life for myself in L.A., with plenty of friends, a sport I loved, work flexible enough so I could goof off at will, and enough qual-ity crime dramas to fill my TV schedule. What was sure to turn me into an unhappy person was spending 130 bucks a week complaining to a therapist about being single. For the cost of one session with a counselor, I could buy six months on match.com. It seemed obvious to me which option was more likely to put an end to the Streak.

While the Therapy Theory crowd felt a solution required some serious soul-searching, another group of my friends insisted the answer was much simpler: I should just stop tak-ing birth control pills. Allan said that over the years he had asked out several women who happened to have just stopped taking the pill. "The moment you're unprepared, it's defi-nitely going to happen," he said. It was true that my birth control pills were going to no use (other than reminding me, on a daily basis, that I wasn't having sex). But to me, going off the pill was the ultimate symbol of giving up, even more so than quitting match.com, and I simply refused to do it.

There was one final hypothesis I knew I had to consider: the "just not cute enough" theory. Okay, nobody actually brought this up to me. Well, nobody except Grandma Ruth, who once asked, "Have you gained weight? You look heavy. Men don't like heavy." (A week later she said, "Have you lost weight? You're too skinny. Men like a girl with some meat on her bones.") I never took this theory too seriously, since there was plenty of evidence in the world that people not considered particularly attractive still found mates. But just to rule it out, I decided to be proactive and have my appearance evaluated on a Web site called amihotornot.com. For no cost, I could submit my picture and let the public rate me on a scale from one to ten.

"Are you insane?" Nancy said. "Why are you going to let total strangers have that much power over you?"

"I'm not giving them any power," I said. "I just need a focus group."

I chose a casual photo of me sitting on the grass wearing jeans and a long-sleeved, sky-blue T-shirt. With the sun highlighting my Angela-straightened hair, the image had a wholesome, Iowa-farm-girl quality. I thought it was relatively flattering.

Since I'm lousy with technology, a computer-geek friend posted the photo for me. When I logged in a few hours later, 116 people had rated me, and my score was not at all hot: 2.7. "You are hotter than 18 percent of the people on this site!" I was informed. A few hours after that, with 864 votes tallied, I was still only a 2.8—in the 19th percentile of hotness. I was devastated.

Now, I was well aware my photo did not possess the three qualities that appeared to garner top ratings on the site: blond hair, major cleavage, and extremely major cleavage. But still. It's not as if I'd posed for the photo in my cycling helmet.

Surely something had gone awry. I asked the geek to check the picture he'd posted, and my instincts proved correct: Some technological glitch had warped my image like a funhouse mirror. He fixed the problem, and I eagerly awaited my revised rating. The next time I checked, I had received a 5.1 rating. After 186 votes, I was in the 45th percentile of hotness! In retrospect, I probably should have quit then, but I got greedy and wanted to see how high my rating would climb. Instead, it started going in the other direction. Within a few hours, I was down to a 4.6—the 41st percentile.

Kate, fretting over what my little experiment was doing to my self-esteem, suggested I post a new photo. "That one doesn't do you justice," she said. "Besides, you should be wearing a tighter top." But taking another photo seemed more trouble than it was worth, and anyhow, I didn't consider myself in competition with the 90th-percentile blonde va-voom girls.

Kate then offered to boost my score by voting for me repeatedly with "ten" ratings. But I declined, since the point of all this was for me to be judged by an impartial jury.

On the verge of dropping below the 40th percentile after 1,932 votes, I concluded the public could turn unjustifiably jaded and pulled my photo. Anyway, I needed to get some work done—something that had proven problematic over the previous three days, since I had been checking my hotness rating at least once every four minutes.

After deliberating on the merits of the various "I'm to blame" theories, in the end I was left with one conclusion: I wasn't guilty beyond a reasonable doubt. Maybe I had, in small ways, contributed to my predicament, but I was satisfied that my singlehood was not, for the most part, self-inflicted.

I also decided it was important to take into closer account who had been proposing the theories. With only one or two exceptions, they all happened to be my coupled-up friends—a fact that made me question whether they were subconsciously examining my life through too harsh a lens. I knew from my own experience that couplehood comes with its own understandable self-satisfaction: When you've found another human being to stamp you with a seal of approval, all the insecurities that come with single-ness quickly fade away. You become utterly convinced that if you could find somebody, then anybody can. So for us "still singles," only one explanation seems logical: Somehow, we've been sabotaging ourselves.

Still, given the grim statistics, I had to wonder if some-thing was askew. Was my predicament really just about bad luck?

Then Cristina, my secretary of outrageous ideas, came up with the most amazing theory of all. The problem wasn't me. It was my condo.

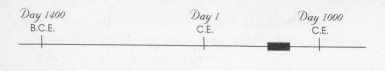

17

Tanked

*F*rom the day I moved in, I thought my condo had it all. The furnishings were stellar, thanks to my sister's decorating talents. The place had plenty of atmosphere, thanks to the recessed lighting, a gift from Dad. And the cabinets were stacked with mustard-colored tablecloths, linen napkins, silver trays, and bread baskets—"in case you throw any brunches," my mother had said by way of explanation for her surprise delivery. My personal favorite acquisition was my satellite dish, which gave me the option of watching *Law & Order* twenty-seven times a week if I felt like it.

Cristina, however, felt the place had one serious problem: an energy imbalance. "You need a feng shui consultant," she insisted.

At first this idea seemed as far-fetched as my trolling for guys at the dump. I was going to attract a boyfriend by rearranging my furniture according to ancient Chinese principles? But Cristina was a believer in the power of feng shui. With her finances in the toilet, she'd hired an advisor to evaluate the energy in her art gallery. After a complete overhaul—including the addition of a gold beam and a purple wall—Cristina's business began to thrive. She'd snagged her first book contract and a lucrative licensing agreement with a floor-mat company. "Feng shui works for relationships, too!" she said.

I was plenty skeptical, not to mention horrified at the prospect of painting my condo purple, but I did like the idea of a solution that didn't involve any awkward coffee dates. After researching feng shui on the Internet, I found a consulting firm that seemed unlikely to suggest anything drastic. "Subtlety is the key here," the company's Web site said. "If your house looks like it has been feng shui'd, then it wasn't the best application of feng shui remedies. Your home should look natural and beautiful, not forced or uncomfortable."

According to the site, I could reasonably expect results to occur within a month. "However, do not expect anything amazing," the site cautioned. "Many times, feng shui does not change the apparent, but rather creates a space that will allow doors to open."

I called and arranged for a $400 consultation. The idea seemed so preposterous that I felt it was bound to work. (Of course, now that I think about it, that's also what I'd said about my move to Bend, my romance with BikeMan, and my pursuit of the redheaded guy.) A few days later a short, slight, stone-faced woman in a gray power skirt suit showed up at my door carrying a black power briefcase.

"I am Lily Wong," she announced, shaking my hand with a death grip. "I am from Hong Kong."

Perhaps sensing my skepticism, Lily offered that she had been studying feng shui for nine years and had taken numerous advanced classes. She then parked herself at my dining room table, popped open her briefcase, and removed two compasses. She explained that authentic feng shui involved complicated scientific calculations to determine the energy characteristics of a building and its occupants and required balancing of the five elements: fire, earth, metal, water, and wood. She warned me against feng shui charlatans who promoted wind chimes, incense, and flutes. After posing a few key questions, including when I was born and when my condo was built, she banished me to my office so she could focus on her computations.

Twenty minutes later, Lily summoned me back for a room-by-room discussion of the "necessary remedies." Overall, she said, the energy in my condo was "so-so," but with the proper adjustments, I could turn things around. The prognosis was good.

For starters, she said, the east side of my condo had an "overabundance of earth," so I would need to move two of my plants in terra-cotta pots to the other side of the entry-way. I would also need to spend more time in the uphol-stered chair in the living room and less time on the sofa.

"But it's a lot more comfortable to watch TV on the couch," I pleaded.

She shot me a look that said, "Do you want a husband or not?" She explained that the sofa was in the north section of the condo, which had only marginal energy, whereas the chair was in the northwest section, which had excellent energy. She also said my bedroom needed more metal. If things got really dire, she said, I should start sleeping in my guest bed-room, which had better energy than my own bedroom.

Then she laid out the single most important remedy: My office needed an aquarium.

"No way!" I said. "I hate fish!"

"You don't need fish," she said. "You need water. Twenty to thirty gallons."

"What about a Sparklett's water dispenser? I was thinking about getting one, anyway."

"No. The water must be circulating and filtered."

"What about a small fountain?"

"No. A fountain only holds five gallons. You must have twenty to thirty."

"What will happen if I don't get an aquarium?"

"I cannot say. But I found my husband three weeks after my mentor recommended I purchase two aquariums for my bedroom."

Enough said. I paid Lily and she left, but I was still feeling conflicted. On the one hand, buying an aquarium for my office seemed ridiculous. How was I going to explain a fishless tank of water to visitors? On the other hand, what did I pay the woman four hundred bucks for if I was going to ignore her advice?

I called Cristina about my quandary. As it turned out, we had hired advisors who practiced very different varieties of feng shui. Cristina's consultant was more progressive, she said, whereas I got a more fundamentalist consultant—"like Jerry Falwell or one of those Orthodox Jews with the long beards." Nevertheless, Cristina felt I should implement Lily's suggestions. I considered hiring a second advisor, but at $400 a pop that seemed excessive. Plus, I worried that I might be forced to choose between two sets of recommendations. What if I chose the wrong one?

I decided in favor of the aquarium and roped Allan, my jeweler friend, into shopping with me. (It wasn't tough. Like anyone who makes a living from home, he was always looking for an excuse to avoid work.) Our first stop was a pet store in my neighborhood, where I found a sleek plastic model for $110.

"What kind of fish are you interested in?" asked the store's teenage employee, who sported a variety of lip and nose rings.

"Well, actually, I'm just looking for an aquarium," I said sheepishly. "It's a long story."

"Oh, feng shui? We get a lot of that."

I was stunned. Here I thought I was doing something really exotic and innovative, but unbeknownst to me, I was actually a cliché.

Though slightly demoralized, I was still committed to buying an aquarium, but I didn't want to purchase the first one I saw. So next Allan and I went to Petco, the Wal-Mart of pet stores, where we found a slew of bargain tanks for $25. I told the salesman I was looking for an aquarium that held twenty to thirty gallons.

"Feng shui?" he said.

"Is it that obvious?" I replied.

The salesman asked whether I had been professionally consulted or whether I was going the self-help route. I could at least hold my head up and say that I had been advised by a pro.

"You're lucky to get away with buying just one aquarium," he said, shaking his head. "The other day some lady came in saying she needed two hundred and fifty gallons of water, for three different rooms in her house. I had this other customer who was advised to fill in his swimming pool and build a new one on the other side of the house. But then he got divorced and hired a different feng shui consultant, who said he needed water right where he had filled in the old pool. So he built an even bigger pool where the old one was. I don't know what happened after that."

The salesman led me to a tank that was the perfect size for my office but held only eighteen gallons of water.

"My advisor specifically told me I need at least twenty gallons," I said.

"Why don't you just take the sticker off?" he suggested. "She'll never know the difference."

"But I'll know. What's the point of doing all this if I don't do it right?"

Besides, I thought, if I don't find a boyfriend, I might always attribute it to the missing two gallons of water. Meanwhile, I was feeling uncomfortable about buying a bottom-of-the-line aquarium. Allan agreed it was a bad idea.

"If you get a cheap tank," he said, "you might end up marrying some lowlife loser."

Ruling out Petco, we went to a high-end store that sold custom-designed aquariums built into wall-sized cabinets.

"What do these run—about five hundred bucks?" Allan asked the salesman.

The man sneered back, as if Allan had offered that amount for a Matisse. "Actually," he said, "between six and seven thousand."

He sized us up pretty quickly as nonclients and suggested we go to a pet store "where they'll sell you a cheap aquarium and then get you on the expensive fish that die right away."

We ended up back at the first store, where I purchased the sleek model, along with a pump and filter, for $159 plus tax. We then drove to my condo and filled the tank. I was too embarrassed about the fishless aquarium to put it in plain view, so I hid it on the floor, between my desk and the wall. The pump made a low-level humming noise and the bubbles gurgled audibly, but after a few days I found the sounds to be kind of soothing. Amused by my latest venture, Kate bought me a miniature plastic deep-sea diver. "You can't just have *nothing* in an aquarium," she said.

I was prepared to wait a couple weeks for results, but much to my surprise, my luck improved immediately. At a charity fund-raising luncheon that very week, I won a $500 gift certificate to a Beverly Hills clothing boutique. A few days later I placed second in a bike race, my best-ever finish. Maybe things were finally going my way.

Valentine's Day, a week after that, was even better. I went to dinner with a cyclist named Garth, a friend of Allan's who was visiting from their hometown in Canada. Allan had dumped Garth on me so he and his wife could have a romantic evening, and remarkably, Garth and I hit it off. He was tall and handsome and athletic and funny. Sure, he lived in another country, but so had Allan when he'd met his wife (in Montana, where both were vacationing). My first date with Garth went so well that I was certain there would be a second, the distance notwithstanding. A few days later, in an e-mail from Canada, he even mentioned the possibility of a future rendezvous at a ski resort.

I was on an emotional high from all this good fortune when I ran into my downstairs neighbor, Catherine, in the garage we shared. We joked about how tough it was to fit both of our large cars in such a small space. "When they built this building in 1946, they sure didn't anticipate sports utility vehicles," she said.

"What?!!" I shrieked. "The building was built in 1946? My escrow officer said it was built in 1948! I'm certain of it!"

"No, it was definitely 1946," she said, noticeably puzzled about why I would care. "My parents were living here back then." I now had a serious problem on my hands. According to Lily, the year of construction was a crucial aspect of feng shui calculations. When I'd told her my condo was built in 1948, she had said, "Are you *sure*? This is very important."

What if this mistake had thrown off Lily's entire evaluation? What if the aquarium was supposed to hold forty gallons of water? What if it was supposed to go in the living room? What if I wasn't supposed to buy an aquarium at all?

I didn't know what to do. Call Lily and ask her the consequences of this mistake? What if she charged me $400 for a second consultation? This was nothing short of disaster.

While I was debating what steps to take, my good luck ran out. In my next bike race, my legs failed me, and it was all I could do to avoid finishing last. Then Garth lost interest in me, apparently mistaking my initial burst of enthusiasm for something far more serious than potential Streak-breaking. He retracted the ski-vacation idea, and I never heard from him again.

Not only had my aquarium apparently driven away a potential Streak-breaker, but now it was pissing off my neighbor.

"Do you have a water purifier?" Catherine asked tersely one day when we met up in the garage.

"No, why do you ask?"

"Well, there's a humming sound coming from your office."

"Oh, it's my aquarium!"

"Well, it's so loud that I can't sleep. It sounds like a BMW is idling outside my window."

Clearly, feng shui was not working. After three

months—somewhere in the high six hundreds of the Streak—I scooted the aquarium to the bathroom, used a pitcher to empty the water into the tub, and carried the tank to the storage locker in my garage, placing it next to the snowshoes I'd bought in Bend.

At this point, I realized, I had exhausted all explanations—rational, semirational, and barely rational—for why I was in such a dating slump. All my reflection, research, and experimentation had left me more perplexed than ever, and a bit concerned, too. What if I was destined for significantly protracted singleness? What if I hit one thousand days? What if I reached *two* thousand?

But then it dawned on me: Those were entirely the wrong questions to be asking myself. Since at this point, I was doing all I could in my search for a mate, why expend any more energy dwelling on it? I decided I would be better served by focusing on something that was clearly within my own power to change—namely, the never-ending routine I was stuck in. Riding my bike, having lunch with friends, screening profiles on match.com, writing articles like "Maximize Your Metabolism"—my life had become more dreadfully dull than *My Dinner with Andre*. Maybe there was something worse than "still single". . . still single—and *boring*.

There was still a huge gap in my life—a gap I'd spent nearly two years searching for a man to fill. But stepping back, trying to gain some perspective on my situation, I had to wonder: Why was I waiting for someone else to give me a sense of fulfillment? Weren't there other goals in life besides finding a guy?

Something had to change. In a really big way.

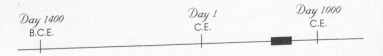

Day 1400
B.C.E.

Day 1
C.E.

Day 1000
C.E.

18

Mission: Implausible

There had, of course, been other times in my life when I'd felt the need to do something drastic, like when I'd quit my job at the fitness magazine to cycle across the country and when I'd quit my life with Alec and moved to Bend. But those were mere distractions compared to what I needed now. It was time to venture much farther outside my comfort zone.

Predictably, my mind leapt to my catchall response to any problem: leaving town. I had to admit the idea was appealing, and I had more frequent-flyer miles than I knew what to do with, having charged every burrito and stick of gum I'd bought in a decade to my United Airlines Visa card. But my most recent experiences with distant travel hadn't been especially satisfying. There was Kenya, of course. And just two months before, I had fled to Reykjavík, Iceland, for the sole purpose of avoiding the requisite dinner my family would be having to celebrate my thirty-third birthday. ("Sorry, Mom, can't make it—will be at the Hotel Sjomannaheimilio

Fjolsklduhusio!") I'd chosen this destination mainly because Icelandair kept bombarding me with e-mails touting bargain fares, and also because I could arrange to arrive in the morning, after a red-eye from New York City. What easier way to get through a birthday than to spend it in a deep, jet lag–induced slumber?

I'd tooled around Reykjavík, taking in the geothermal swimming pools, the seafood restaurants, and the art galleries; but my heart wasn't in it. Once I was back in L.A., I could see there was an obvious reason why: I'd traveled thousands of miles with no greater intent than to escape. If I was really serious about shaking up my life, I knew I needed to do it with a sense of purposefulness. I was in the Barnes & Noble travel section looking for inspiration one day when I ran across a book called *Volunteer Vacations,* which promoted the idea of combining travel with good works. Suddenly, amazingly, it all clicked. I could make myself useful to society! And I could travel while doing it! What—besides, of course, a happy, long-term relationship with great sex—could possibly be more fulfilling? This was exactly what I'd been searching for: an ambitious plan to fill the Void.

Granted, being useful was going to be a tall order for a person with no altruistic instincts or practical skills. Up until now, my contributions to the betterment of the world had been minimal. I'd never worked on curing some dread disease, building a brighter future for children, saving the whales or the redwoods. For my latest magazine assignment, "The Ultimate Butt Workout," my editor had instructed me to address, among other issues: "What exactly do women want in their butts? Higher? Tighter? Rounder? Lifted? Stronger? What muscles make up the butt? Can you do anything to get the dent? Why are some butts more bubbly while others are flatter? Is it tissue? Genetics?"

Obviously, I was not going to be winning any Pulitzers for public service.

The truth was, I had managed to live thirty-three years without developing competence in a single area that could serve anyone but my cellulite-obsessed readers. Aside from that, I was utterly clueless about any concept that began with the phrase "do-it-yourself." I could not, say, caulk a window or trim a hedge. I'd never sawed a board, drilled a hole, or replaced a washer. For that matter, I wasn't exactly sure what a washer was.

Not that these deficiencies were entirely my fault. After all, I'd been raised by two people who together couldn't change a furnace filter. When I got my new California license plates after moving from Bend, my father was the one who asked, "When are you going to take those to the shop to get them installed?"

Over the next few days, I began to formulate an ambitious strategy for self-improvement. I would put my 256,808 frequent-flyer miles to good use and travel the world as a freelance volunteer, funding the venture by flying home periodically to work overtime cranking out fitness articles. The essential first step, of course, was to come up with an official name, à la Lollapasuza and the Streak. It was Kate who finally had the inspiration, albeit unintentionally. After I'd filled her in on my plans, she laughed much harder than even I thought was justified and exclaimed, "So what are you going to call this—'Mission: Implausible'?"

I had to admit it was perfect. While my sister was interviewing wedding coordinators and arranging her schedule of engagement parties and showers, I would throw myself into planning an itinerary for M:I. I decided to use the wedding—six months away—as my end point. Clearly, I didn't have the constitution or the bank account to volunteer indefinitely, and if one of the by-products of my excursions was being absent from all the prenuptial planning, well, who was I to mind?

Perusing books and surfing the Web, I was stunned to find literally thousands of exotic and enticing volunteer opportunities. I could clean rivers in Greenland! Farm eggplants in Japan! Teach English in Lithuania! Rehabilitate raptors in Kentucky! Repair steam trains in Wales! Build houses in Ghana! Each venture I came across sounded more exciting than the last, and I soon became so overwhelmed by my choices that I knew from experience that I was headed for trouble.

Back when I was a newspaper reporter, I covered an ice cream tasting contest that required participants to sample four dozen flavors, only a few of which would survive the journey from research lab to supermarket freezer. When the sponsors invited me to taste the flavors, too, I knew I had found my dream assignment. Standing in a room full of giant ice cream tubs, I plunged in. But sadly, I failed to pace myself, began to confuse Kona Coffee with Almond Roca (or was it Mocha Fudge?) and, after sampling forty-eight flavors of ice cream in a two-hour period, developed severe stomach cramps. Then, in an ill-considered attempt to neutralize the sugar overdose, I ate an entire box of bacon-flavored crackers and a package of Italian salami. I spent the whole night moaning on the couch, and it was months before I tasted ice cream again.

I knew I did not want to suffer a similar fate with

Mission: Implausible. I needed to gather my wits and formulate a sensible and manageable plan. If I couldn't do everything, then at least I could do a handful of different things. Diversity, I concluded, would be the key. I'd volunteer in the United States and abroad, help animals as well as humans, experience big cities and rural villages, work indoors and out. I'd try organized expeditions that I paid for, along with volunteer programs willing to accept my services for free.

Meanwhile, I had to be mindful of my limitations. Although the point of all this was to stretch myself, I didn't want to take on more than I could handle. What if, due to my shoddy workmanship, some Fijian bungalow collapsed, killing a family of eight? Unlike, say, half the preschools in New York City, most of these volunteer organizations didn't have much of a screening process. They'd take almost anyone willing to show up, qualified or not. So I had to decide for myself if I was up for the challenge.

I concluded I'd offer my services for relatively short periods, so as not to unduly burden these wonderful organizations with my ineptitude. I figured, How much damage could I inflict on any man, woman, or raptor in a matter of weeks?

From the ice cream calamity, I knew I also had to schedule breaks between missions so that I would not burn out on being useful and risk never volunteering for anything again, other than booking the spa treatments for my friend Cami's bachelorette party. I'd have to come home periodically, anyway, to write my fitness articles. Plus, I did want the opportunity to pursue any match.com possibilities that might surface. Although I had downgraded my expectations for Jen's wedding from steady boyfriend/possible mate to presentable escort, I wasn't about to completely abandon my search.

To help me select specific missions, I consulted with my few friends who had actually done some good themselves. My Kenya friend Julie recommended a nonprofit group that monitors elections in Zimbabwe, but I decided I'd rather focus on programs where potential bodily harm was more likely to involve lower back pain than, say, multiple stab wounds.

Another useful friend, a former Peace Corps volunteer who ran an inner-city community center in Dallas, suggested Heifer Project International, an Arkansas-based antihunger organization where she once spent a week extracting fecal samples from goats. "Don't worry!" she said. "You wear really long gloves!" In a rare moment of bravery, I actually did call the Heifer folks, who cheerfully accepted my offer to volunteer but said I'd have to commit to at least one month on the farm. I had no idea what kind of drugs they were taking.

I also made an inquiry about a sea turtle conservation project near Savannah, Georgia, dedicated to monitoring the habits of these endangered creatures and their hatchlings. My duties would involve being stranded for a week on a sweltering island and waiting up every night for the remote possibility that a turtle would crawl ashore. After sunrise, I'd retire with my group to a stifling, showerless cabin and attempt to sleep on a cot.

When I was told that the program was sold out all summer long, I was relieved that the turtles could survive without me.

I also tried to sign up for an archaeological dig of woolly mammoth bones in South Dakota, figuring I could do little harm to animals that were not only dead but also extinct. Alas, this project was sold out, too.

Who knew this volunteer thing was so popular?

While assembling my itinerary, I attempted to explain the concept of M:I to my family. Their reactions were not unexpected.

"How are you going to make any money off this?" Grandpa Julius demanded to know.

"I certainly hope you're not planning to climb up on any scaffolding," Grandma Honey said.

At this point, Grandma Ruth was in such failing health that she didn't really understand what I was talking about. All she said was, "Bring me home some chocolate."

My parents, by now accustomed to my unpredictable nature, offered their usual support—"That sounds fabulous, hon!"—but the way they said it sounded like they'd just come up for a quick gulp of air before resubmerging themselves in my sister's wedding preparations. My sister and John were also encouraging but otherwise preoccupied, primarily with getting my mother to trim her fourth cousins off the guest list.

So finally, after researching hundreds of volunteer opportunities and eliminating projects that involved cleaning rodent cages, speaking Polish, or administering anesthesia, I had devised my itinerary.

My first stop: Fairbanks, Alaska, where I would be serving as a volunteer for the six-day, 267-mile Midnight Sun Ultra Challenge, the longest wheelchair race in the world. My mission: to drive a pilot car for one of the athletes, trailing him during the race to protect him from traffic. Given my affinity for athletic competition, I was really looking forward to this trip, although the confirmation letter I received in the mail did give me some pause. "You are responsible for the safety of your athlete," the letter said, "and the maintenance of your vehicle." Considering my dubious vehicular history—twice I had driven off at a gas station with the nozzle stuck in my fuel tank and three times I'd scraped my Trooper while pulling into my garage—seeing "responsibility," "maintenance," and "vehicle" in the same sentence caused me a bit of concern.

Still, I was undaunted. Setting off on my first mission, I felt my life was about to take on new purpose.

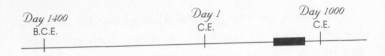

Day 1400
B.C.E.

Day 1
C.E.

Day 1000
C.E.

19

Voluntarily Committed

Sometimes in life, it's easy to determine what's useful and what isn't.

Writing "Total Cellulite Makeover": not very useful.

Grandparents reminding me I'm not married: very not useful.

Protecting wheelchair athletes from becoming roadkill: useful.

Relying on wheelchair athletes to change your flat tire: criminally not useful.

As you can surmise, my first venture into the realm of volunteering did not prove to be an unmitigated triumph. On the upside, I did manage to keep Mike, the wheelchair athlete assigned to me, both alive and safe, fulfilling the first half of the duties outlined in the confirmation letter. However, I proved less successful with the maintenance of my Daewoo Leganza, the rental car provided by the event planners. In my defense, if something was going to go wrong, don't you think it's better that it was with the car?

No doubt my low point in Alaska came the morning the rear tire on my Leganza went flat, a discovery I made just twenty minutes before the day's race was scheduled to begin. Having no clue how to go about fixing it, I just stood and stared at it in disbelief. A few minutes later one of the racers, a studly blond twenty-four-year-old, wheeled by and assessed the situation. Looking at me, then at the tire, then back at me, he shook his head and said, "Man, I really don't want to get down on the gravel to change this thing," which he promptly did. I would describe this scene to you further, but I was so mortified I could do nothing but stand aside and tie my shoes repeatedly.

I suppose I could also go into detail about the speeding ticket, the fender bender with the motorhome, and the time I let Mike's wheelchair roll into oncoming traffic in downtown Anchorage. But hey, why humiliate myself unnecessarily when the bigger point is, lest I repeat myself, that Mike was still alive and well at the end of the race?

I had arrived in Alaska primed to become the new Useful Me, woman on a mission—raring to go, to get things done, to make a difference. But by the end of the race, I knew I had to reassess any hopes I had for my usefulness potential. I realized this around the time of the race's award ceremony when the event director, after handing out several thousand dollars in winnings, announced there would be one more prize.

"And this"—he paused to hold up a blue and yellow tin—"goes to the volunteer who best personifies what I am holding right here. Suzanne Schlosberg, come on up and get your *Spam*!"

Yes, I had won a twelve-ounce can of the most ridiculed item in luncheon meat history, awarded, the director went on to explain in so many words, to the volunteer who proved to be the most entertaining without totally fucking up. As I walked toward the podium to accept my can of mysterious pork product, my fifty fellow volunteers apparently not as surprised as I was, I can't overstate my sense of accomplishment. Here I was, on just my first foray into good works, and already I'd been honored for making an impact, albeit unintentionally.

I was definitely off to a good start, but flying home from Alaska, I knew I didn't have much time to bask in this newfound glory. Within days, I would be off to Papua New Guinea, a tropical island nation north of Australia, where I would join a volunteer crew to help construct a Habitat for Humanity house. Driving a car fifteen miles per hour was one thing; wielding an actual construction tool was something else entirely. If I couldn't even change a tire, I had serious concerns that I could actually build a house.

As it turned out, though, I found myself in good company. Every member of our all-female group displayed an aptitude for construction that was perhaps a half-step above the Tinkertoy level—a fact that must have befuddled the residents of Sisi, the village we were assigned to. Though we were treated with supreme hospitality throughout our visit—the villagers worked mightily to feed us, welcomed us into their church, and serenaded us at mealtime with native songs set to acoustic guitar—I could not escape the feeling that what they were really thinking was, "Who the fuck *are* you people?"

Early on, I mentioned my concern about our incompetence to our group leader, Janie, but she was unfazed. She said she intentionally excluded men from her work teams because they tended to dominate the job site with their construction experience, leaving women little to do. Unconvinced, I began to suspect the real reason was because the presence of men would have increased the likelihood that *someone* in the group would have been productive, and Janie might have been shamed into actually working, rather than roaming the construction site shooting photos of the local children.

Fortunately, our construction supervisor, Kaimo, was a man of infinite patience. Even though it was obvious that our group was actually slowing down their home-building efforts, he instructed his men to hold the lumber in place and allow us to do the sawing and hammering, rather than vice versa. Jeffrey, the villager assigned to hold my planks, seemed to get a kick out of the arrangement. He would chuckle when I'd mangle a nail, then take my hammer, bang the nail straight in with a couple good whacks, and hand the hammer back, putting the whole shameful process in motion again.

The village women were so fascinated by my group that when they weren't preparing sweet potatoes or washing pots and pans, they would stand on the perimeter of our construction site, watching us as if they'd just tuned in to the latest episode of *Survivor*. One of the women became so exasperated by my ineptitude that she impulsively grabbed my hammer and straightened the nail herself. Half a dozen seven-year-olds gathered nearby burst into laughter.

As the days passed, I redoubled my determination not to leave the villagers with a permanent impression that American women are useless idiots, and my construction skills did eventually rise to nondisaster levels. But still I felt certain the house would have been built faster if our group had never shown up. It wasn't as if the Habitat for Humanity release forms had required us to take the

Hippocratic oath, but still, shouldn't the most important rule of volunteerism be "first do no harm"? Once again, I took my discouragement to our leader, Janie.

"You're completely missing the point," she responded.

She went on to confide that, in reality, our mere presence was our most significant contribution to the construction of the house. Sure, the village men were more capable, but without the novelty of our being there, they wouldn't even have been motivated to show up to work.

"So, basically, we're like car show models?" I said.

"You could say that," she replied.

The paradox of this revelation—our inherent uselessness actually proved useful—was at first a bit unsettling. I suspected I would not have signed up if the brochure had said, "Participants will display their lack of construction skills in order to lure male volunteers to the job site." But then I began to sense a trend. Just like in Alaska, I had become an unwitting provider of comic relief. There are worse things a volunteer can do, eh?

I was also starting to see an unexpected bonus to this whole volunteering business. One afternoon, as I was swatting away mosquitoes during a brief work break, it dawned on me that I'd completely lost track of the Streak. Whereas at home I had devoted countless hours trying to master the intricacies of match.com, now I was completely preoccupied trying to master the handsaw, not to mention the six-step process involved in using the bee-infested pit that was our latrine. (Step Five: Rearrange your village-mandated floor-length skirt, then tell yourself, "Suck it up, Suzanne," before straddling the hole.) The prospect of going dateless to my sister's wedding was the least of my concerns.

Not that there was any Streak-breaking potential on any

of my missions, just in case you're wondering. Obviously, the Sisi expedition was a washout in the male department, but none of the other missions offered even the most remote prospect, either. Virtually every other volunteer I worked with was in a demographic that collects either Social Security or facial piercings. But then if I'd thought about it before-hand for two seconds, I would have realized that makes perfect sense. People with jobs and mortgages and three-year-olds aren't going to spend what little extra time and money they might have digging water wells in Cameroon. Surprisingly, learning that there were no eligible guys in vol-unteerland was somehow affirming. At least I knew that I hadn't been looking in the wrong places all these years. Clearly, all the good men weren't off being do-gooders!

After my first two missions, I could see that my origi-nal plan—filling the Void—was seriously not happening. Discovering you have unintended entertainment value just isn't enough to inject a new sense of purposefulness into your life. But as a way of distracting myself, M:I was turn-ing out to be a bonanza. Incredibly, I had stumbled upon a way to earn an excused absence from my family's altar-altered state. At the Schlosberg family gatherings between missions, I'd regale everyone with stories of my misadven-tures, but the moment the talk threatened to turn toward wedding videographers or rehearsal dinner hors d'oeuvres, I could say, "Gotta run. Time to go make myself useful!"

As if that weren't incentive enough to get out of town, during my hiatus after Papua New Guinea, I endured one of my most insufferable match.com predates. Justin was a graphic designer, and I had found his smile appealing enough initially to turn on approximately sixty-three per-cent of my charm. But then we had this little exchange:

Justin:	So do you enjoy gardening and cooking?
Me:	Well, actually, I'm a serial plant killer, and the only kitchen appliances I know how to use are my toaster and my blender. But I'm really good with the blender!
Justin:	(smirking) Well, don't you think it's about time you got in touch with your domestic side?
Me:	Don't you think it's about time *you* got in touch with your polite side? (I didn't actually say that last part.)

Afterward, I couldn't imagine a bigger waste of my time. But then at that point I hadn't endured my next mission—a two-week experience that made me question whether there was something even worse than bad blind dates and no sex.

This mission, at a chimpanzee research institute in Washington state, consisted of (1) two days of scrutinizing slides and videos so we could learn how to distinguish the five chimps on site, (2) two days of lessons and tests on an inexplicably elaborate code used to record the chimps' activities, and (3) five days of watching the chimps, who, despite being surrounded by such curiosities as floral handbags, hairbrushes, Halloween masks, and *Vogue* magazine, did virtually nothing.

I never was able to surmise whether the chimps had decided to take a sabbatical from the research during my stint, or perhaps they'd gotten wind of my group's test scores and decided minimal activity was all we were capable of properly documenting. But by the end of the mission, I didn't especially care.

Drained from the tedium, I left the comic relief to one

of the other volunteers, Colin, a gray-haired, fifty-one-year-old British police officer who expressed no interest in either chimpanzees or Washington state. He had come solely as a favor to his wife, Margaret, to whom he referred, affectionately, as "my little coil of barbed wire" and "my little ice bucket."

"The decision was simple," Colin later told me. "If I hadn't come, she would have divorced me."

I thought that was terribly sweet.

Throughout our time together, Colin kept me entertained with his extensive repertoire of expressions of torment, pointing his fingers to his head to suggest a handgun, pretending to slit his wrist with his pocketknife, making loud snoring noises, or saying things like, "I think I'm going to go stick pins in myself."

Other than that, the whole chimp experience was so unbearably mind-numbing that one day I was shocked to realize I actually yearned to call my sister and find out whether she'd finally picked a flavor for her wedding cake. Of course, it did occur to me more than once that I could just bolt the mission. But with a determination comparable to what kept me going on that disastrous Death Ride, I somehow managed to last to the end. As Nietzsche would have put it if he'd volunteered at the institute, what does not kill you from boredom makes you stronger.

If anything, the chimp institute was a lesson on just how grand life was back in L.A., dateless and sexless though it was. But I couldn't quit M:I on such a dreary note, let alone give up on a concept in which I had invested so much time. If my sister was going to achieve everlasting marital bliss, I at least had to prove I could be useful. So after a couple more mediocre predates, I was more than ready to plunge into my next mission. This time I headed for Xi'an, China, a city of six million where the smog is so thick that you can actually see and feel it, like dry ice vapor on a dance floor.

My task was to teach conversational English to boarding-school students who, it turned out, didn't speak a word of the language. From my volunteer group's initial meetings with the school's English teachers, who could hardly say "good morning" themselves, it was obvious that any "conversations" we might be having with the students would be more akin to charades. The sign on the school's gate hinted at the challenge ahead: "The Outside Traffic Is Forbiden."

My first few days with the students proved less than productive, but I felt I could lay part of the blame on my team teachers, two retired pastors named Fred and Walter, whose classroom style seemed tied specifically to their need for reassurance of their own superiority.

"My name is Teacher Sue," I said, introducing myself the first morning to a class of smiling sixth-graders, figuring "Suzanne" was going to be pushing the outer limits of their pronunciation skills. "I live in America."

Then Teacher Fred said, "I live in San Diego, California, on the west coast of the United States. What do you know about San Diego? Sea World? The zoo? Ever see the Chargers play?"

He then lobbed an imaginary football across the room.

The eleven-year-olds turned their heads to follow the imaginary pass, then turned back in befuddlement. Fred went on to describe the benefits of living in Southern California.

Another day I taught fifth-graders with Walter. "My name is Walter Rowe," he said. "You might think it's pronounced 'Row,' as in 'row your boat.' But it's really pronounced 'Row,' rhyming with 'cow.' If you saw the word 'R-O-W-E,' how would you pronounce it?"

To preempt the impending awkward silence, I whipped out a J. Crew catalog I'd brought from home and attempted a lesson on colors.

"This is a red coat," I interjected. "This is a green shirt."

Walter groaned and whispered to me, "Can't you at least find a plaid shirt? Let's teach them 'plaid.'"

On the forty-five-minute bus ride back to our hotel, I fretted about how little we were getting across to our students, who always seemed on the verge of lapsing into a coma. But Fred and Walter only gushed about how fortunate the children were to have met us. "They've probably never even *seen* an American before," Fred said. "This is the chance of a lifetime for them."

By the second week, I was able to jettison the undynamic duo and teach a class myself. I remained undaunted in my determination to contribute in some way, especially once I got a look at the sixties-era British textbooks that were being foisted upon my students on a daily basis. I wasn't fully aware of the suffering that goes on in China until I learned firsthand that twelve-year-olds were being forced to read the following: "Mr. James Scott has a garage in Silbury, and he has just bought a garage in Pinhurst. Pinhurst is only five miles from Silbury, but Mr. Scott cannot get a telephone for his new garage, so he bought twelve pigeons. Yesterday, a pigeon carried the first message from Pinhurst to Silbury."

Once I realized how dire the situation was for these students, I racked my brain for some way to help. One afternoon I tested out my solution du jour: tongue twisters focusing on "th," the sound that gives the Chinese the most trouble. I wrote on the board: "Martha and Arthur went to the theater at three-thirty on Thursday." Then I turned toward the class and made a motion like a symphony conductor. In joyful unison, the class said: "Marser and Arser went to za seeter at sree-sirty on Sursday."

My strategy was a hit! For the first time, the students weren't slumping in their desks or chatting with their friends in Chinese. They actually burst into giggles! When I feigned distress over their mistakes, I really put them in stitches.

"Noooooooo, it's not *S-S-Sursday*!!!" I'd say, covering my ears as if to block out the sound of a dental drill. "It's *Th-Th-Thursday*!!!" Then I strolled the room and demanded that the students stick out their tongues through their teeth and say, "Th-th-th-th-th-th."

Of course! Why hadn't I thought of this before? If my only proven usefulness to date was to serve as entertainment, it made sense to play to my strength.

For the next several days, my lesson plan consisted solely of tongue twisters. My single greatest contribution to the youth of China was the one that popped into my head while I was reading *Glamour* on a lunchbreak. Back in class, I held up the magazine, motioned toward the slender blonde on the cover, and said, "Courtney Thorne-Smith—famous American actress!" Then I pointed just below Courtney's miniskirt and wrote on the board: "Courtney Thorne-Smith has thin thighs."

The students happily stumbled through it as if they had mouthfuls of marbles. But my favorite student—a small, serious boy who had worn the same brown-and-beige sweater for eight days straight—tried with all his might to get it right. Scrunching his eyelids and furrowing his brow as if he were doing calculus in his head, he came closer than anyone else, including his teacher, who had studied English for twenty years.

"Courtney Thron-Smith has thin sighs," he said quietly.

"Fantastic!" I said. "Great job!"

A couple days later, after the entire class had filed out of the room on my final afternoon of teaching, my little sweater guy stayed behind, standing silently while I packed my bag. Then he followed me down three flights of steps without saying a word. As I turned to leave the building, he tapped me on the leg and, making sure I noticed his tongue was sticking through his teeth, said softly, "Thank you, Teacher."

Heading home, I finally felt I was getting the hang of volunteering, and I decided the time had come to fly solo. Abandoning the organized missions, I put out the word, mostly on Internet bulletin boards, that I was looking for a genuine opportunity to make myself useful and would fly anywhere in the United States to do it. (My frequent-flyer account was still overflowing.) I politely turned down the unemployed lawyer in Virginia who wanted me to help find her a job, as well as the Arizona woman who sought my help in collecting one hundred million signatures to protest animal cruelty in Korea. But I couldn't possibly turn my back on Becky Tegeler, a first-year elementary-school teacher in Nebraska.

"Come to our school for a week!" Becky wrote. "Try to help writers who are ten years old and still can't spell, and reach the very gifted kids who bore easily . . . Experience firsthand poverty in Middle America, the last place people think to help out when they want to really 'do something.' You would be more useful here than perhaps anywhere else in this nation."

Confident that children found me at least amusing, I showed up a few weeks later at Hartley Elementary in Lincoln to serve as volunteer spelling test giver, recess monitor, and show-and-tell item. Clearly, Miss Tegeler's class of fourth- and fifth-graders had been instructed to act as if they were beside themselves with joy over my visit, but it was obvious they had no idea why some lady from California who wasn't even a teacher would fly all the way to Nebraska to help them put commas in their sentences.

Most of the boys remained standoffish through the week, but the girls quickly abandoned their puzzlement and took a liking to me. They even confessed they hadn't been looking forward to my arrival.

"I thought you were going to be an old lady like the type that goes to church all the time," Jasmine owned up.

"No offense," said Mary, an aspiring gossip columnist, "but I thought you were going to be like Miss Goody Two-shoes."

No offense was taken. I quickly learned that "no offense" was Mary's favorite expression. She had already told me, "No offense, but your gray sweatshirt is boring" and "No offense, but your hair is kind of thin."

It wasn't long before the girls had attached themselves to me as if I were a five-foot-seven piece of Velcro. Pigtailed Sally clung to my right leg wherever I walked. Kaitlyn, one of the shyer girls, gave me hand massages, while Kascha, the tallest in the class, kept her arm wrapped around my shoulder. All of them exhibited an insatiable curiosity about me.

"Are you married at all?" Jasmine asked one day at lunch.

"Nope," I said. "Not even a little bit."

Mercifully, unlike my grandmothers and crazy Willie at

the Jackpot casino, Jasmine didn't seem the least bit alarmed about my single state. She just shrugged and moved on to her next line of questioning, demanding to know the names of all the chimps I'd met at the institute. I'm not sure whether Jasmine understood why I gave her a little hug, but she hugged me back.

By the end of the week, Miss Tegeler's kids had definitely made an impression on me, and I decided it was time to pull out all the stops and try to leave an impression on them. Around 10 A.M., a representative from the cafeteria staff stopped by and announced that the lunch menu would feature two items: chicken nuggets and foldinis. At the mere mention of "foldinis," Miss Tegeler's entire class plunged into mass hysteria, as if they'd just been offered boiled pig eyeballs.

A foldini, I should explain, is essentially a piece of pizza folded in half—sort of like a calzone, only smaller, flakier, and, well, stinkier. Foldinis were so feared and loathed by Hartley students that earlier in the week, long before anyone knew they'd appear on the menu while I was in town, I had been warned that their grossness was off the charts. Even one of the teachers had told me that students had reported finding dead insects in their foldinis. He imparted this information in the same tone used by TV anchors when they report suspected UFO sightings, that sense of "Hey, it's possible—maybe these people aren't completely nuts."

After the students placed their lunch order—all thirty-four of them screamed, "Chicken nuggets!"—I announced, for purposes of heightened suspense, that I would be postponing my decision until lunch period, when I could actually sniff and inspect a foldini. I had every intention of ordering one because—was this selfish or selfless?—I confess: I wanted to be remembered as the Lady Who Ate the Foldini.

At lunch, I was lucky enough to be invited to join a table of six girls, including Jasmine and Mary. When our table was summoned to the cafeteria line, the girls grabbed their chicken nuggets, then stood there, wide-eyed, awaiting my decision. I had to admit the foldini had a certain warmed-over stench, but I wasn't deterred. When I told the girls I was leaning toward the foldini, I caused an all-out frenzy.

"Oh my gosh, that is *so* disgusting!" Mary shrieked, jumping up and down. "Once there was a foldini that had *five flies* in it!"

When I returned to the table with my foldini, all the girls watched in astonishment as I took my first bite.

Now, before I offer my impressions, I should probably mention that I have a history of tolerance for institutional food. While my college friends fled the dorms after sophomore year, I gladly spent nine semesters on the university's twenty-meal-a-week plan. Even the weakest link in the menu rotation, the rubberized hamburger, served every other Saturday for lunch, was superior to anything my mother ever cooked while I was growing up.

Still, even a person with a more discerning palate would have had to concede that the foldini was hardly the gastronomic version of Frankenstein's monster that I had been led to believe. True, it was almost cold and perhaps not as chewy as it could have been, and the filling was a bit sweet. But I encountered no flies, dead or alive, and contrary to predictions by the girls, I did not feel even the slightest urge to barf. But I didn't let on to the students, since I was, after all, aiming for hero status.

As I popped my last bite, Mary squealed, "She did it! She ate a foldini!"

The girls were so impressed by my courage and so

amazed I was not going to succumb to a slow and agonizing Death by Foldini that they talked of nothing else all afternoon.

A few minutes before school was out, Miss Tegeler gathered the whole class for a wrap-up of my visit. I decided to use the opportunity to get some feedback on my performance and asked the students to rate my usefulness on a scale of one to ten. At first they all shouted, "Ten!" But it was obvious they were just trying to please Miss Tegeler. When I told them that I knew full well I did not deserve perfect scores, my ratings began to plummet.

Mary dropped hers to an eight and a half. "No offense," she said, "but you were just *kind* of useful."

That sounded like a fair assessment to me, not only of my visit to Hartley Elementary but also of the entire M:I endeavor.

Day 1400
B.C.E.

Day 1
C.E.

Day 1000
C.E.

20

Fast Times at Starbucks

*E*ven though you're much too polite to ask, I'm sure you're wondering what it's like to be in a dry spell that has hit the high triple digits. I completely understand—morbid curiosity is only natural—so let me give a go at explaining.

Yes, of course, you're consumed by lust, if not 24/7 than at least 24/6. (The feelings tend to fade on the days you spend among the eighty-plus crowd at your grandparents' assisted-living facility.) Sometimes you catch yourself having thoughts that are, if not criminal, then at least totally inappropriate. For example: You're lifting weights at the gym and your eyes focus on a tall, V-shaped guy doing squats, and you think "Hmm, *that* guy has a nice ass"—and then you realize that, in addition to having a nice ass, the guy probably has chemistry homework, since he looks to be in the eleventh grade.

Naturally, fantasy sex is a predictable response to your situation, and unlike M:I, this was one area where I had no trouble becoming a proficient do-it-yourselfer. But here's the strange thing: Even though, in your fantasies, you can imagine having sex with anybody you want—that is, after all, why they call it a *fantasy*—you find yourself imagining sex with guys you aren't especially attracted to and sometimes with guys you actually dislike, and you realize to your horror that your imagination is doing what you swore you would never do: settling.

Here's another odd thing: Even though you desperately want sex, you can't actually remember what sex feels like. It's sort of like knowing that you had to-die-for tiramisu that summer in Tuscany, but for the life of you, you can't remember how it tasted. To the best of your recollection, you enjoyed sex immensely. You must have—didn't you?— or why would you be craving it so much now?

Sometimes, you fear that you've forgotten *how* to have sex. What if, like a car that hasn't been started in several years, when you finally get the opportunity, you won't "turn over"? When I've shared this concern with my friends, they've brushed me off with lines like, "Believe me, you'll know what to do. It's like riding a bike." But this is no comforting analogy to me. Once, after a long cycling layoff, I lost my instinct for twisting my cleats out of my pedals and toppled over at a stoplight, sustaining an injury I will not describe other than to say that it required a visit to the gynecologist.

When you're in the midst of an epic celibacy streak, you have little patience when people complain about their own, less heroic dry spells. Once, flipping through a magazine in a checkout line, I ran across an article titled "Could You Give Up Sex for Forty Days?" The subhead: "Would you last a day? A week? A month? We asked five women to summon their willpower, fend off their partners, and take a vow of celibacy for forty days." Forty days! Such fortitude!

Such sacrifice! Such determination! What would next month's featured story be: "Could You Give Up Shopping for Twenty Minutes?"

When you haven't had sex in forever, you find yourself behaving horribly to your single friends who complain that their boyfriends aren't attentive enough or committed enough or are obsessed with the wattage of the subwoofer on their surround sound home-entertainment system. Even given your own misery, you still hate yourself for responding, "Yeah, but does he have a penis?"

You're even more impatient around married people who complain that they "never" have sex with their spouse, by which, of course, they mean (1) never as much as they want it, or (2) never as much as they used to have it, or (3) never as much as they believe their single and Streakless friends have it. But "never" doesn't actually mean *never*. This is an especially common complaint among couples with infants. But if you do the math, you will see that even someone with an eight-month-old is still—worst-case scenario—well under the six-hundred-day mark. (And just doing the math means you have now sunk to a new low of one-upmanship over the issue of *not* having sex.)

Mercifully, my fixation on my sexless predicament was held to a minimum throughout the whole M:I venture. In fact, if I'm going to be brutally honest, I have to admit that the person who benefited most from M:I was me—not in the "you'll get more than you give" sense implied in the heartwarming volunteer literature but in the sense that, for six entire months, I stopped thinking of myself as a candidate for the Celibacy Hall of Fame.

The extent to which M:I had been an elaborate escape, from both my dry spell and my sister's prenuptial planning,

didn't truly hit me until an acquaintance who knew nothing about the Streak asked, "So what sort of volunteering
will you be doing now that you're home? There are so
many great opportunities right here in L.A.!"

I must have looked at her cross-eyed. It was such an obvious question, but not once had it occurred to me to continue
my good works after I returned home for my sister's wedding.

"Do you think I spent six months and two hundred
thousand frequent-flyer miles just to get out of going to
Jen's engagement parties?" I asked Nancy later.

"You're just figuring this out *now?*" she said. "Your
scheme was brilliant—on par with the Jews in Poland who
went underground during World War Two."

Successful though it had been, the scheme, of course,
couldn't go on indefinitely, and once M:I was over, I found
myself in the exact same place where I'd left off. Despite
several Starbucks dates during the pauses between my missions, I was still no closer to finding a companion for my
sister's wedding.

With the wedding now just weeks away, my family was
in the final frenzied stages of the launch sequence.
Everyone's latest panic was that too many people would
RSVP and the hotel ballroom wouldn't be able to accom-
modate all the guests.

"Why don't you guys just show it on closed-circuit TV
in the lobby?" I suggested, offering to give up my seat and
watch the simulcast instead.

Nobody seemed amused.

Despite the guest list crisis, my mother somehow managed to keep open the option for me to come with a date.
"Let me know if there's anyone you'd like to bring!" she
offered more than once.

I knew if I was going to find a date, I'd have to come up with someone quick. And then, with remarkable timing, a friend told me about a new concept in matchmaking that couldn't have been more tailor-made for my quandary. It was called Speed Dating.

Here's how it worked: A group of fourteen singles—half men, half women, all around the same age—would meet at Starbucks, and the organizers would pair everyone off. You and your "date" would have eight minutes to chat; then a bell would ring and the men would rotate to the next table. At the end of the night, you'd turn in a card with "yes" or "no" checked next to each person you'd met. If any matches were made, the organizers would notify you the next day.

I learned from the organizers' Web site that Speed Dating was created to foster Jewish marriage, and only Jews were allowed to participate. That was fine, but the main draw for me was the musical-chairs format. Everything about Speed Dating just seemed so time-, cost-, and labor-efficient. How could you possibly run out of things to say in eight minutes? And an entire date would be shorter than the uncomfortable good-bye that tends to cap off full-scale blind dates. (Saved by the bell—what could be better?) The fee was only fifteen dollars, certainly less than my Frappuccino tab for seven separate dates. And Speed Dating was a snap compared with all the screening, profiling, and e-mailing I'd done on match.com. Maybe getting thrown in a room with seven random guys was actually a better way to go. Maybe plain old luck was more powerful than research.

Nancy was appalled when I told her I'd signed up. "Isn't that awfully cynical?" she said. "How can you possibly dismiss someone in eight minutes?"

I thought about the number of guys I could have dismissed in eight *seconds* and decided that eight minutes was plenty of time, if not to decide whether there was an actual spark then at least to see whether there was a possibility. If match.com coffee dates were "predates," these would be "pre-predates." Of course, even the chance of a spark might be hard to detect in a few short minutes, so I'd need to come prepared with just the right questions—probing but not prying, lighthearted but not silly, specific but not confining. As usual, I turned to my friends for help, but I'm not sure how seriously they took the assignment.

"Are you a heroin addict?" was one suggestion that arrived via e-mail. Among the others:

"How many singers are in the Kingston Trio?"

"When was the last time you went to a live sex show?"

"Are you ready to go home and meet my family this afternoon? I think my grandmother's really going to like you."

"How many nights a week do you envision yourself watching *Law & Order*? Who is your favorite assistant district attorney on *Law & Order* and why? If you could take just one season of *Law & Order* to a desert island, which season would it be? (Specify by cast, not year.)"

Clearly, I was on my own in this endeavor. Ultimately, I came up with a half dozen questions that I felt would pinpoint the guys' interests and aspirations. I had the list in my pocket when I arrived at Starbucks, which had been rented out just for our group and so lacked its usual hum. The fourteen of us stood around awkwardly, coffee beverages in hand, eyes darting about, clearly aware that we were participating in an unusual social experiment but not saying much besides, "So, how'd you hear about this?" Given the format, it somehow seemed that talking to anyone outside of the allotted eight minutes might offer an unfair advantage, and—

I'm only guessing here—nobody wanted to be perceived as a cheater. As I scanned the room, none of the guys immediately caught my eye, but I was ready to keep an open mind.

Our session was led by a cheery rabbi who didn't look much older than our twenty-five to thirty-five group but who assumed the air of a relationship guru, although from what I could tell, his primary qualification seemed to be that he was married and we weren't. He explained the rules and told us we were allowed to ask our dates anything except (1) Where do you live? and (2) What type of work do you do? This, he said, was to ensure that we wouldn't make snap judgments based on "superficialities." I guess I could buy the first exception (although "with my mother" or "at the halfway house" would have been important information to know). However—excuse me?—when did choice of career become superficial?

As far as how the evening went, allow me to offer a few choice excerpts:

BACHELOR #1, MITCH

Distinguishing characteristic: Uncanny resemblance to Danny Bonaduce in the later seasons of *The Partridge Family*.

> Me: So, what's your ideal Saturday?
> B1:   What do you mean?
> Me: Well, if you could do anything you wanted on Saturday, what would it be?
> B1:   But I always have to work on Saturdays.
> Me: Yes, but *ideally*—if you *didn't* have to work— how would you spend, say, this coming Saturday?

> **B1:** Well, the date would definitely involve nineteenth-century European architecture, with a lot of fountains, and a beautiful woman. We would read poetry for three or four hours and then make passionate love next to the fountains.

BACHELOR #2, JOE

Distinguishing characteristic: The habit of pinching the bulge of fat hanging underneath his chin. Also, exceedingly small, pudgy hands.

> **B2:** So, what kind of food do you like?
>
> **Me:** Pretty much anything except sushi. I love Mexican, Italian, Thai, Indian . . .
>
> **B2:** So what do you usually order when you eat Mexican?
>
> **Me:** You really want to spend our eight minutes discussing tacos?

BACHELOR #3, ARI

Distinguishing characteristic: Excessive cologne.

> **B3:** Man, I just had this bitchin' conversation with that girl over there about music. She knows all these alternative bands that I like.
>
> **Me:** How great for her. For both of you.
>
> **B3:** Yeah, I was totally psyched. She even likes Throbbing Gristle. They totally rock. Like, you have no idea.
>
> **Me:** You're right, I have no idea!

BACHELOR #4, BRETT

Distinguishing characteristic: None.

I have no recollection whatsoever of the eight minutes we spent together.

The first four dates were followed by a break, at which point I was starting to doubt that Speed Dating would put me on the fast track to acquiring a date for the wedding, let alone getting laid. I didn't think anything was wrong with eight-minute dates—at this point, I was immensely grateful for the time limit. But the experience did remind me why, a year earlier, I'd instituted my Three Reasons policy, requiring, as you may recall, that my friends name three solid reasons—not counting Jewish and single—that any prospective date and I might hit it off.

During the first four "dates," the rabbi had roamed the room with his hands folded, cocking his head this way and that, like a fourth-grade teacher supervising a math test. Now, at the break, he suggested that our conversations weren't probing deeply enough. "Ask more provocative questions!" he said. "Ask your dates, 'What are your top three priorities in life?'" And so we began again.

BACHELOR #5, AARON

Distinguishing characteristic: Limp handshake.

Me: So, like the rabbi said, what are your priorities in life?

B5: (long pause) Well, I guess one of my priorities is to figure out what my priorities are. You know, find a direction.

Me: What kind of direction?

B5:   Like, you know, whether the Torah was writ-
      ten by God.

Me: Do you have any other priorities?

B5:   Health. Health is important.

Me: Absolutely! So what sort of exercise do you
      do?

B5:   I walk around. I mean, I'm not going to go to
      some gym where everyone thinks they're
      God's gift or anything like that.

Me: Well, is there anything you'd like to ask *me*?

B5:   Yes, as a matter of fact. What's your definition
      of kindness?

Me: Well, I suppose it's when you go out of your
      way for someone, even if it's inconvenient for
      you. What's your definition?

B5:   Respect. Like when you're nice to the people
      who work at Starbucks and don't act like
      you're better than them, even though—I
      mean, come on, they work at *Starbucks*.

BACHELOR #6, MICAH

Distinguishing characteristic: Enough gel to make his hair
look like it was made out of plastic.

Me: So, where do you go on vacations?

B6:   Vacations?

Me: Yes, you know, like when you take time off
      from work?

B6:   Geez, I can't remember the last time I did that.
      But I'll probably go to Vegas after I graduate

law school, since I probably won't have another vacation for at least twenty years.

BACHELOR #7, ELI

Distinguishing characteristic: Acute overdependence on "freakin'" (see below).

> Me: So what were your favorite movies in the last year?
>
> B7: I just saw *The Patriot*—it was freakin' awesome. How about you?
>
> Me: I loved *Election*. I laughed so hard my stomach hurt.
>
> B7: Holy shit, I hated that movie. It was so freakin' stupid. I should've asked for my money back.
>
> Me: Well, did you see *High Fidelity*? I thought it was hilarious.
>
> B7: Jesus Christ, it's like *enough* with this John Cusack guy. Does he have to be in like *every* freakin' scene of *every* freakin' movie?

When the bell sounded for the seventh time, I knew time had run out. I would be going dateless to my sister's wedding.

Day 1400
B.C.E.

Day 1
C.E.

Day 1000
C.E.

21

~~~~~~~~~~~~~~~~~~~~~~

Old Maid of Honor

As far as I've been able to deduce, betrothed couples tend to fall into three general genres: (1) the Romantics, who dedicate themselves to creating the most unforgettable, most perfect, and of course, "happiest" day of their lives; (2) the Troopers, who look upon the months of grueling preparation as a boot camp of sorts, figuring if they can survive the seating-arrangement battles and bridesmaid-selection trauma, the marriage will be a snap; and (3) the Pragmatists, who make a few thoughtful decisions to create a special if modest day that is simply a starting point to their new lives together.

When I imagine plans for my own wedding—which I try not to subject myself to with any frequency, given my prospects at the moment—there is no doubt I fall into the third, no-frills category. I'm seeing a small, intimate gathering, maybe even an elopement at a mountain lodge; a dress with considerably less square footage than a parachute; and a brief but loving exchange of vows followed by a low-key reception (after which the bride and groom adjourn for long, hot, sweaty honeymoon sex—but perhaps that's another fantasy).

The weddings I've attended that were planned by Romantics have almost invariably turned into dicey affairs, with so much attention paid to the event that the marriage itself became almost an afterthought (a couple of them didn't last as long as the engagements). What's more, so much pressure was put on that single day to be "perfect" that any little glitch was elevated to catastrophic proportions, inspiring comments such as, "The (pick one: best man who got plastered, low-cut dress worn by the groom's mother, rabbi who forgot our names) *ruined* our wedding."

By far, the most typical wedding I've witnessed has been planned by a Trooper couple. Just as there's some unwritten law that children must beg to go to Disney World and high-school students must rent limos for their senior prom, so are engaged couples seemingly obliged to do certain things to earn their marriage. These affairs follow the same basic script: 150 to 200 guests, an upscale hotel, matching sea-foam green bridesmaids' dresses (clearly chosen with the approval of the maid of honor, whom the style flatters much more than the other bridesmaids), a slightly awkward first dance (suggesting the bride and groom did not graduate at the top of their prenuptial waltz class), a really loud band that plays "R-E-S-P-E-C-T" and "Margaritaville," a table-hopping tour by the bride and groom, the newlyweds feeding each other cake, a bouquet toss, and so on.

Despite all the agony and exhaustion that typically precede these events—I've heard firsthand accounts that make Navy SEAL training seem like a breeze—they typically come off just fine, and ultimately, all the tensions are forgotten, never to be talked about again. Although I wouldn't want one of these weddings for myself, they seem to serve their purpose well. At least I can say that all my friends who have had them are still married.

It wasn't until I began to absorb the intricacies of my sister's wedding that I realized there is a fourth nuptial genre: the Performance Artists. These are the couples who look upon their special day not simply as a ceremony or celebration or time-honored tradition, but as an opportunity to make some sort of creative statement. For all I know, Jen and John may be the only members of this category, but they certainly set the bar for any who follow.

Granted, this sort of wedding was in keeping with their personalities. John was an actor, and Jen had, after all, been a performance artist. After her "Party as Performance" college thesis, Jen went on to enlist several dozen Volkswagen Beetle owners to drive in different formations in a parking lot—the red ones going one way, the greens going another, the blues parked with their doors ajar and hoods popped open. A newspaper dubbed it a "Bug Ballet."

Jen was determined not to have a cookie-cutter wedding, and John was wholeheartedly supportive of her determination. No, my sister wasn't going to do anything outrageous, like cartwheel down the aisle naked; her creativity was tempered, as always, by her impeccable sense of style. But certainly there would be no generic hotel, matching bridesmaids' dresses, or heart-shaped truffle boxes on the tables. The black-tie affair would begin at L.A.'s oldest and most majestic synagogue, with nine bridesmaids and nine groomsmen dressed in formal attire of their choosing, then continue at L.A.'s grooviest hotel, a 1920s art-deco landmark with a grand staircase, magnificent chandeliers, and breathtakingly high ceilings.

Other than the fact that all of this was costing barely less than the gross domestic product of Malawi and was turning virtually everyone related to me into candidates for Thorazine, if not electric shock treatment, I thought it was okay. But it was Jen's eight-page, three-thousand-word, full-color booklet that I felt took the whole business of "making a statement" far too literally. Copies of this booklet, a chronicle of Jen and John's formative years and relationship, were to be placed at each table setting at the reception, intended as keepsakes for the guests. Jen had written a touching reminiscence of their milestones—their first date, John's conversion to Judaism, Jen's conversion to cat lover, John's momentous visit to Angela, our hairdresser, who cut off his shoulder-length hair with the snip of a ponytail. But the booklet also included segments that were not so heartwarming. For instance, their first big fight and the progress of their collective therapy sessions—his, hers, and theirs.

Once my mother and father read the draft of the booklet, they went through the roof. If my parents are about anything, it's decorum, and the way they saw it, the booklet was suffering a lack of it. When my mother suggested to Jen that a wedding reception was not the place to "air dirty laundry," my sister accused her of wanting to "ignore reality."

"People need to realize a wedding is not a fairy tale!" Jen fumed. "Relationships are hard work! We've overcome a lot!"

My parents and sister opened negotiations over the wording, but talks quickly reached an impasse. Naturally, Jen turned to me for empathy and support. That's the way it had always been for us. Despite our innumerable differences, we'd never had any trouble maintaining a united

front whenever our parents were (depending on the situation) overreacting, oblivious, irrational, or insane. On a fairly
regular basis we referred to them as Those People (as in,
"Can you believe Those People hated *Pulp Fiction*?"), so I
knew exactly whom Jen was referring to when she called to
complain that the booklet was under threat of censorship.

"Just so you know, Those People are like Mr. and Mrs.
Jesse Helms," she said, sputtering with rage.

Looking back, I realize there are many ways I could
have chosen to respond. "Yeah, I can't believe how obnox-
ious they're being," for instance, or "I know—it's completely outrageous. It's your wedding, and you should be
able to say whatever you want."

But, the truth was, I felt this time my parents weren't
insane. It didn't seem to me that our friends and family
needed Jen and John to point out that relationships take
effort. I mean, isn't that just a given? Perhaps it would have
been worth the ink if they'd had to overcome some life-
threatening disease or had lost all of their possessions in a
flood. But did anyone really care how much therapy they'd
been through? Their close friends already knew, I figured,
and my grandfather's cousin Meyer from Missouri could
easily have been left out of the loop.

"If mentioning all the therapy upsets them so much," I
told my sister, "then why not just take it out? What's the
big deal?"

She hung up on me. I had broken the cardinal rule of
siblinghood: Never take your parents' side in an argument.
And thus began the Cold War.

Of course, this incident wasn't solely responsible for the
hostilities that ensued. Relations between Jen and me had
been deteriorating for months with the widening of the

inevitable chasm that develops between the singular and the plural. My situation with Jen certainly didn't introduce me to this phenomenon—I'd been going through it with some of my girlfriends for years—but looking back, I can see how Jen's wedding became kind of emblematic of all those other experiences.

The chasm starts out as nothing more than a crack—a small, almost undetectable fissure. The two of you might even make vows that you won't let her new relationship change the friendship. But no matter what, little by little, you begin to feel the distance between the two of you grow.

Yes, you still communicate, but now conversations are restricted to work hours or e-mail. Late-evening calls are out—either she's just not answering or, if she does, you get the feeling that she's otherwise occupied. When the two of you do talk (which is usually at your initiative; what used to be a 50:50 you-to-her call-initiation ratio becomes more like 90:10), her conversation is dominated by the plural, as in, "We're so burned out on California Pizza Kitchen" or "We love our new gym—the elliptical machine is our favorite!" You're baffled: At what point did she stop having her own opinions?

Also, the major bonding issue between you and her—commiseration over the distresses of dating—no longer applies, so you end up conducting perfunctory interviews with each other. ("How's work?" "How're your folks?" "Have you seen that new Denzel Washington movie?") When your dismal dating life does come up, you notice that, sympathetic as she tries to be, she isn't really tuned into what you're saying, exhibiting that eighty-five-percent comprehension rate you get when talking on the phone to people you know are simultaneously reading their e-mail.

Of course, in addition to talking less, the two of you also see each other less. The only time she suggests going out to dinner or a movie is when her significant other is away on business or camping with his buddies. If you call her to get together, she can't commit without preauthorization—a process that, with all the you-her-him-her-you phone tag, can take up to forty-eight hours and usually results in her squeezing you in three weeks from Saturday for a quick lunch at a restaurant in her neighborhood.

On the rare occasions when the three of you get together, it's usually weird, although not as weird as when you receive birthday cards that say, "Love, Cindy and Dan," even though you've met this Dan guy twice. Your singular life is so far removed from their plural reality that they respond to your stories as if you were performing some sort of comedy routine. Granted, you may be going after the laughs, but still . . . it is *your life*.

After a few years of this, let's face it: Any shared intimacy and empathy that existed between the two of you is now in serious decline. Worst-case scenario, the singular-plural chasm can turn a perfectly good friendship into the yearly receipt of one of those "Love, Cindy and Dan" birthday cards.

Jen and I hadn't neared that point by the time her engagement rolled around—not that your own sister could drop so far out of your life, especially if your family, like mine, convenes more often than Congress. But the fact was, by the time we stopped speaking to each other, she was three years removed from the single life and had not been without a boyfriend for even one day during her thirties. The Great Divide had reduced what little communication we were having into brief, tension-ridden exchanges that basically boiled down to her wondering why I couldn't be overjoyed about her wedding, and me wondering why she thought I could.

In retrospect, I probably asked too much of her to understand why, rather than travel with my family to Kansas City for her third wedding shower, I decided to spend the weekend riding my bike and reading a book on theories about the JonBenet Ramsey murder. Being equally removed from her plural way of life, I assumed Jen would excuse my eye-rolling and accept my preoccupation with Patsy Ramsey's clothing fibers. After all, Jen had a fiancé and eight other bridesmaids to lavish her with attention.

But, of course, she couldn't have understood my situation—how could she? All Jen knew was that her wedding was the most important event in her life, she was putting every ounce of effort into making it special, and her sister was being a bitch.

Considering how distressed I was in the final weeks leading up to the wedding, I was expecting to have an epic meltdown on the big day. But the strangest thing happened: I woke up that morning in almost a zombielike state. Overnight, I seemed to have developed the remarkable psychological condition that occurs during extremely traumatic situations: I'd checked out. As I contemplated the day ahead, the wedding seemed less like a catastrophe than a chore—like folding my way through an exceedingly large pile of laundry.

I didn't fret that much about how I looked, which definitely did not qualify as fabulous. My outfit—a sleeveless red sequined top and floor-length red velvet skirt along with low, made-for-comfort black velvet heels—wasn't especially flattering. I'd chosen it, on a shopping expedition with my sister, because (1) it wasn't terrible, and (2) it was what I happened to be wearing in the dressing room of Saks when my watch struck 1 P.M., and three hours was as much time as I could stand to spend in the department stores of Beverly Hills.

Given the colorful cast and all the preproduction hype, you may be wondering exactly how this whole performance came off. I regret to report that given my zombielike state, I'm unable to offer an authoritative review. I can't recall my sister—or myself, for that matter—walking down the aisle or the rabbi holding forth or my parents beaming, as they must have been, as Jen and John exchanged vows. Nor can I remember the floral arrangements that I'm certain looked like they'd popped off the pages of *Town & Country;* nor the other bridesmaids' dresses, which I know were stunning; nor the exact number of relatives who sidled up to me afterward and said, "When's it going to be your turn?" (although I can assure you there were plenty).

What little I do remember comes to me in brief, disjointed flashbacks. Among the most vivid: at the synagogue, before the photo shoot, my sister shrieking, "My dress! My dress!" as if it had just been set on fire. I think the crisis may have had something to do with a hem. (My sister, by the way, had finally settled on a Japanese designer in New York, who handmade a tight-fitting, beaded chiffon gown with spaghetti straps and a long train.)

Also: Jen and John making their first postceremony appearance, hand in hand, at the top of the hotel's red-carpeted staircase, Jen wearing elbow-length white gloves and a mink stole she had rented for the occasion, waving to the crowd à la Jackie O.

"Does she think we're the paparazzi?" I overheard one guest say.

I remember being onstage, toasting Jen and John in front of 220 people, while thinking how odd it was that I, the maid of honor, had made it through the entire wedding without once speaking to the bride. (We never did speak during the reception, either, although I'm sure nobody noticed in all of the commotion.) I also remember that my status in the wedding pecking order spared me from the torment of the room's requisite Singles Table. Instead, I was surrounded by a phalanx of friends and cousins. A good part of our evening was spent reading the booklets, which seemed to reflect a compromise between my sister and my parents: therapy was in, but mentions of fighting were toned down.

As for my grandparents, not only did they manage to stay alive for the affair, but—this much I remember—Grandpa Julius and Grandma Honey were at the top of their game. From the passenger seat of his Mercedes, stuck in the long procession of cars in front of the hotel, Grandpa unleashed, in earshot of the desperately overworked valet attendants, the loudest, most profanity-ridden monologue heard anywhere since Richard Pryor blew himself up freebasing cocaine.

Later, at the reception, Grandma Honey gave what remains, to date, the lengthiest speech of her life, not one word of which I recall. I do, however, retain a vision of her laughing hysterically at her own jokes, playing to the crowd as if she were Joan Rivers doing her Vegas lounge act. Only Grandma Ruth, poor thing, was denied any pleasure at the affair. Sadly, her health had declined to the point where she was propped up in a wheelchair, no longer possessing the strength or the spirit to remind me, as I'm certain she would have liked to, that I was both older than my sister and unmarried. Her eyes were so glazed over, I must say she was more of a zombie than I was.

What I do remember clearly, and with great astonishment, was waking up the morning after the wedding feeling like Tim Robbins after he'd just escaped from Shawshank Penitentiary. The teeth-grinding anxiety that had consumed me for the better part of sixteen months had vanished almost instantly. All I felt was great waves of relief. This only confirmed my conviction, which I'd explained to my sister more than once, that it was not her marriage that was doing me in; it was her wedding.

Surprisingly, my family moved past the event with lightning speed, as well. I had expected everyone to carry on for months about the fabulousness of it all. But just two days later, with Jen and John honeymooning in Mexico, the rest of us got together for lobster to celebrate my aunt's birthday, and the wedding was barely mentioned. I've rarely heard it spoken about since.

The only thing that carried over, unfortunately, was the stony silence between Jen and me. Even after her return from Mexico, neither of us showed the slightest inclination to concede an inch, let alone reconcile. A month later Grandma Ruth passed away, and Jen and I did not exchange even a glance at the funeral. As I sat in the chapel listening to her masterful speech about Grandma Ruth's favorite pastime—lounging by the pool in her bathing suit, slathered in suntan lotion, cigarette in hand—I wondered how long our standoff would last. It seemed absurd to be so estranged from your only sister—didn't that sort of thing happen only on *Jerry Springer*?—but I suspected it would be a good while before we would be calling each other up to complain about our parents again.

By now, I was in the mid nine hundreds of the Streak, edging perilously closer to something I once thought would have been impossible for me: one thousand days without sex. For weeks I'd been so caught up in the chaos of the wedding that I hadn't dwelled on how close this landmark was. But now it was staring me right in the face, and reality was setting in: This was one big fucking number. The sheer enormity of it was about to take me into a whole new caliber of celibacy, sort of like when a tropical storm is upgraded to a hurricane.

When I mentioned to one single girlfriend that I was only a couple months away from the thousand-day mark, she actually praised me for my stamina. "You know, when it comes to sex," she said, "women are like camels: They can go long periods without any." But eventually, she cautioned, "They need to replenish or die." I was fairly certain I wasn't going to actually expire if I didn't get laid soon, but I knew it was time, yet again, to go to the well—match.com.

Even though the service had so far failed to produce a bona fide contender to break the Streak, I never doubted the concept. I suppose I could have gone the route of the more traditional matchmaking services, but the few people I knew who'd tried them out had had distinctly underwhelming results. Besides, I couldn't see paying upwards of a thousand dollars to have some stranger pick my dates on the basis of interviews, questionnaires, and gut instinct. I preferred to trust my own instinct.

This time around, with the wedding pressures gone, I was feeling more confident about the whole process. I'd become so adept at filtering profiles that it was no longer a time-consuming, brain-draining endeavor. I raced through them like a pro, with the skill and intuition to spot trouble (or potential) at a mere glance, the way a radiologist can detect the slightest ligament tear on an MRI. Plus, I was feeling lucky. It somehow seemed fitting that I would survive the wedding alone only to meet a great guy right afterward.

As proficient as I was becoming at spotting potential, however, there were droves of other match.com members who were not so savvy. I'm not sure what it was about my profile that suggested, to a twenty-three-year-old called HereIAm, the potential for a positive response to "You are extremely hot! If I pay you $500, would you have sex with me? I will pay cash up front before we do it. I can go higher than $500 but would have to pay by check as I don't want to carry around more than $500 in cash."

Until this point, I hadn't actually considered prostitution as a way to break my streak, but what an opportunity! I could have sex *and* get reimbursed for my three years worth of match.com fees!

Then, from a forty-six-year-old former paratrooper, I received a poem titled "The Lover's Bath." Allow me to share an excerpt:

> Slowly lower yourself
> to the water, like the quiet book returning
> to a shelf in a library.
> To the soul, soap is peonies in October.
> Do not let your soap dissolve faster than time.
> Refrain from crossing your legs
> and extending them over the tub's lip,
> for this leaves
> a promiscuous shadow on the ceiling.
> Think of my name as your towel.

In general, I was considerably more successful with guys I contacted rather than guys who contacted me. I actually went to coffee with three prospects who, affirming my profiling skills, were quite normal and bright, and all three asked me out on a second date. For various reasons I declined—basically, the chemistry just wasn't there. But things did seem to be headed in the right direction.

Then, with about fifty days to go, I found my first reason to hope since the redheaded SEC lawyer at my gym. But this time my optimism seemed more well-founded since, as a member of match.com, the guy was, obviously, single. His name was William, and he was a blond, thirty-nine-year-old university professor who specialized in the philosophy of probability. I had no idea what that meant and was a bit perplexed by the description of a course he was teaching ("Does God exist? Do electrons exist? Should we believe that God exists or that electrons exist?"). But I was intrigued that a guy with a brain like that was also an O.J. murder-case junkie who had tried, in vain, to get a courtroom seat at both the criminal and civil trials. (I'd never been quite so ambitious, but I did own forty-three books on the case.)

When William and I met for coffee, I was amused by his tales about traveling and teaching and thought I detected the teensiest spark. He was a bit on the geeky-professor side, with a near-bowl haircut, slightly pudgy cheeks, and baggy Dockers with button-down shirt and sneakers. But the conversation was lively, and truth be told, even as we were talking I was already imagining us naked in my guest bedroom. (For some odd reason, my Streak-breaking fantasies always took place in my guest room rather than my own bedroom. Perhaps it had something to do with making a fresh start. Or maybe, on some level, I actually believed my feng shui consultant's suggestion that my guest room had better energy.)

When I e-mailed him the next day asking him on a real date, he responded, "Absolutely!" and I imagined further goings-on in the guest bedroom. But William's follow-through was dismal. "I'm afraid I'm booked up (in fact, overbooked; in fact, overoverbooked)," he wrote me, despite expressing how much he looked forward to seeing me. This pattern held for a couple weeks, during which we saw each other just once, for a pleasant dinner at an Argentinian restaurant. Though it went well, he followed up with several more puzzling e-mails about how much he was looking forward to seeing me again once he was able to squeeze me in. At this point I was getting impatient and I sent him an e-mail politely asking why someone who had put himself on match.com was so seemingly unavailable. "May I ask, what gives? Are you secretly married? Are you moonlighting as a security guard?"

William wrote back that, no he wasn't married, but, well, as a matter of fact he *was* seeing someone else. He "wasn't sure" whether I would mind, so he had never mentioned it. I wanted to respond, "So what is the probability of a probability professor turning out to be an asshole?" But I stopped myself.

At this point, with Day One Thousand looming, I conceded that short of a "parting of the Red Sea" miracle, I was headed for this shocking milestone. When I mentioned to my friends that I was searching for a way to commemorate the occasion, some wondered why I felt a need to make a big deal out of it. "Why not just ignore it?" asked Kate, ever the airbag.

That was unthinkable. Did the Reds ignore Pete Rose's three thousandth hit? Did the United Kingdom ignore the Queen Mother's hundredth birthday? What's the point of keeping a tally if the high achievers don't even get recognized? Not that my occasion was anything to cheer, of course, but you had to admit it was somewhat of a stunning feat. Given all the effort I'd expended over nearly three years (granted, effort that had gone toward averting this milestone, but effort nonetheless), it seemed a shame to let my landmark day go unobserved.

An actual celebration, of course, was out. And a self-indulgent luxury item—a splurge on a new bike, for instance—also seemed inappropriate. Instinctively, I knew only one thing would satisfy my impulse: I had to get out of town. Sure, I was back to the same MO, but at least this time I was admitting it. I wasn't going to run off to Samoa under the pretense of wanting to help humanity. Besides, let's not discount the restlessness that accompanies the deprivation of sex at this magnitude.

After I laughingly dismissed Kate's suggestion that I go hang out at a spa to have my pores individually gouged, I still had trouble coming up with an appropriate destination. It's not as if Frommers.com promotes package deals for the sexually disadvantaged. But I kept surfing the Web, and that's when I hit on the Arctic Ocean Ride of Pain, the mountain-bike trip from Fairbanks to Deadhorse. The short plane ride to Provideniya, Russia, was really just an afterthought—what I anticipated to be a quick out-and-back trip. How can you get that close to another entire continent and not put at least one foot on it?

Logistically, I wasn't able to schedule the trip to coincide with the turn of my new millennium. The actual day that the three zeros clicked over on my celibacy odometer, I was in the midst of a weekend cycling competition in Pomona, grinding my way up a nine-mile mountain pass in ninety-degree heat and lung-busting smog. Drenched in sweat and my quadriceps burning, I was still three miles from the top when I squeezed the last drop of Gatorade from my water bottle and had to will my spent, dehydrated self to the finish line. On the upside, unlike one of my competitors, I managed to avoid passing out and having IV fluids administered to me by the paramedics. That evening, I collapsed on my couch in front of a *Law & Order* rerun, too wiped out to really think about the milestone and all its implications.

On day 1,025 I flew to Fairbanks.

Day 1400
B.C.E.

Day 1
C.E.

Day 1000
C.E.

22

A Tale of a Fateful Trip

So. That almost brings us up to where I am now, which is the living room of a concrete-block apartment in Provideniya, looking out on the blanket of fog that has kept us stranded here for a week. I've made quite a few startling discoveries during this time, but here is one of my biggest shockers: I don't know all the lyrics to the *Gilligan's Island* theme song.

I was absolutely certain I did. I'd have bet money on it. I would venture to guess that, as you read this you too are sure you know the words. You're probably already thinking, "Just sit right back and you'll hear a tale, a tale of a fateful trip . . ." But tell me: What comes next? And how exactly do you get from there to "Here on Gilligan's Isle!"

Several days ago, when it became clear that the six of us—the two retired couples, the computer guy, and me—could be stuck here indefinitely, I snapped into cruise-director mode and came up with a bunch of activities for our group to pass the time. Singing the *Gilligan's Island* song seemed especially appropriate, and I thought later we could make up lyrics about our own fateful trip. But when I started to sing, I found that all I could come up with was a series of disassociated phrases—"the *Minnow* would be lost," "uncharted desert isle," and so on.

On the first try, my companions proved equally inept. But four of us were undeterred and spent the better part of two afternoons racking our brains to reconstruct the song. At one point, we switched strategies, abandoning rote memory in favor of logic. Our brainstorming session went like this:

"Okay, you guys, we *know* the skipper was brave and sure, and we know they went on a three-hour tour, but, like, what would have happened in between?"

"Hey, would a ship 'strike' ground or 'take' ground?"

"Think, people. Think!"

Although we're still working on it, we've actually made a lot of progress. But two in our group, Jim and Don, have been less than amused by our Gilligan initiative, as well as by our entire predicament, and they seem to feel their time is better spent bemoaning the unfairness of it all. "My fishing trip in Alaska has been *destroyed*!" is the daily mantra of Jim, a retired art professor from Texas who came to Provideniya for the same reason we all did: because it's there.

But I've been having a swell time. Although the trip was originally just an afterthought, it's turning out to be considerably more fun than the planned centerpiece of my vacation, the Ride of Pain.

I suppose I should fill you in on what has happened since I took off on a mountain bike from Fairbanks. One thing that didn't happen, as you can surmise, is sex. Though

I secretly had fantasies of breaking the Streak in a tent on the tundra, the three men in my group—two over sixty, one twenty-two—did not qualify as prospects. And anyway, as I quickly learned, Arctic Alaska is not a place where you'd want to be showing a lot of skin. The weather wasn't uncomfortably cold, at least at first, but the mosquitoes were so ravenous they chased us as we pedaled down the road. Two days in, my butt already resembled a topographical map of Afghanistan.

Once we left the last tree behind and entered the Arctic Circle, the sun never set and each day was essentially the same. Every morning, with mosquitoes swarming, we'd dismantle our tents at warp speed, then pedal north on gravel for six to eight hours, shutting our eyes every time an eighteen-wheeler would hurtle by and whirl up a tornado of dust, which was about every eight minutes. (The Dalton Highway, a.k.a. the Haul Road, is the only thoroughfare between Fairbanks and Prudhoe Bay, where the Trans-Alaska Pipeline starts.) We'd then erect our tents in a cloud of mosquitoes, and dive in for cover.

Eventually, in the pouring rain, we reached Deadhorse. Though it is probably the least charming spot on the continent—a frigid, windy, treeless, gray hodgepodge of pipeline, tractors, trailers, forklifts, and oil-drilling machinery—I liked the place a lot, primarily because it also houses an abundance of beefy oil workers. The male/female ratio looked to be about 980 to 1. As I wandered the halls of our motel, which was actually a dozen trailers stuck together, I wondered how long it would take me to break the Streak here, if I were to stick around. Alas, I was there hardly long enough to do a load of laundry and catch up on some sleep.

All in all, I was satisfied that the Ride of Pain had commemorated my Thousand Days with an amount of suffering commensurate to the occasion. I then flew to Nome to meet up with the group traveling to Provideniya. I knew almost nothing about our destination, which didn't rate a single mention in the *Lonely Planet*'s 976-page Russia guidebook. Details on the tour company's Web site were sketchy, revealing little more than the fact that the town was the easternmost Russian port in the Arctic and that we would be "meeting with local people."

The first surprise upon arriving in Provideniya, on a nine-seater prop plane, was that there weren't any local people to meet with. Well, barely any. The majority of the town's five thousand residents had fled after the Cold War ended, the military pulled out without bothering to take their machinery with them, and the place began to fall into ruin. We were told that some sixteen hundred people had stayed behind, but the town seemed more like an empty set from *Mad Max*.

As Yuri, our wiry, good-natured guide, gave us a walking tour the first day—"This is factory—doesn't work. . . . This is hotel—doesn't work. . . . This is bank—doesn't work. . . ."—the seven of us looked at each other sideways as if to say, "Good thing we're only staying two days!" Yuri also pointed out the one building that did function: the public bathhouse, open twice a week for men and twice a week for women. It's the only place residents can get a warm shower because, otherwise, there is no hot running water. I've been once; the showers work fine, but I wasn't keen on the full-body mauling I received from a big, blond woman who apparently felt I hadn't washed myself thoroughly and spontaneously started scrubbing me with her

Brillo pad. As she did, it occurred to me that Kate was getting her wish for me after all—the whole experience was distinctly reminiscent of spa torture.

Our home for the duration is the three-bedroom apartment of a zaftig retired schoolteacher named Nina—whom Yuri calls "Five Stars Nina" since she is Provideniya's one-woman hotel industry. The morning after our second night at Nina's, we packed our bags, only to be informed by Yuri that the airport was closed due to fog. Every day since, we have relived some version of that morning, and every day, too, Yuri laughs when we persist in asking questions that Provideniyans know better than to waste their breath on. For instance: "How can the airport possibly be closed on weekends?" "How can it take a whole day to fix one downed power pole?" "How can they cancel the entire day's flights just because there's morning fog?"

I haven't been one of the main inquisitors. In fact, the only question I've asked on a daily basis is "Can we go to the gym?" Yuri had pointed out the dilapidated gymnasium on our walking tour, and once we were officially stuck here, I was curious to see if there was any workable equipment inside. A few others seconded the motion. Yuri, who's more of a cigarettes-and-vodka guy, seemed to think it was a nutty idea. But he has kindly cut through the red tape that makes even a trip to the rec center a bureaucratic challenge, and he now babysits us there for an hour or two in the afternoons, since for some reason we can't be left alone. (Going for a jog or even a brisk walk is impossible, by the way. There are only four streets in town, forming an obstacle course of potholes, yawning cracks, wooden planks, and giant piles of rock.)

Turns out the gym doesn't have much in the way of

equipment—a few jump ropes, dumbbells, broken-down weight machines, and really strange free weights that look like bowling balls with handles. But I adore the place. The other day I spent a good two hours teaching dumbbell exercises to a dozen eight-year-old Russian Inuit girls who are also stranded here. Residents of an outlying village, they've been camped out at the gym while waiting for the airport to open so they can go on a government-sponsored vacation to a city west of here. Thrilled for a diversion, they insisted I keep showing them new exercises. I finally ran out of ideas and was reduced to demonstrating wrist curls. (To date, I've never been assigned a story titled, "Stronger Wrists by June!")

Eventually, we moved on to arm wrestling—the gym has one of those professional desk-type tables you see on ESPN2 "Strongman" competitions. At some point a boy who looked to be about seventeen walked in, sat down at the table to await a challenge, and before I knew it, my little weightlifter girls were clapping and cheering, "SU-zanne! SU-zanne! SU-zanne!" Determined not to let the girls down, I used every bit of strength I had to outlast the guy with my right hand—it took several tense minutes to break our deadlock—and then, on pure adrenaline, I took him down in a matter of seconds with my dominant left. The guy slunk out of the gym without catching my eye, and the girls flocked around me as if I were Muhammad Ali after he'd just thrashed Joe Frazier in the Thrilla in Manila. Obviously, my entertainment appeal had remained intact since M:I.

When we're not working out, working on the Gilligan project, or teaching Yuri American slang (yesterday the retired couples introduced him to "you're pulling my leg," while I taught him "no fucking way") there's always time to play Scrabble. Several days ago, I fashioned a board and some tiles from scraps of yellow paper and duct tape I found in the apartment. I know I didn't get it exactly right. Despite all those years playing with Grandma Ruth, I couldn't recall the placement of all the Double Word scores or how many Rs and Ps and Ds there are. But the Provideniya Edition works. At first, enthusiasm among the group was low, but when I pointed out the options—staring at the fog or watching the only show on TV, a Brazilian soap opera dubbed in Russian—a couple of them agreed to play, mostly, I think, to shut me up. But the game has caught on big-time. This morning I chuckled when one of our group members who initially scoffed at my board finished breakfast and said, "Scrabble, anyone?"

As each day has passed, and my spirits have soared higher, I've had to wonder what's come over me? I mean, it's not as if being stranded in an Arctic ghost town is a natural recipe for a good time. The moods of the others have ranged from calm acceptance to resignation to downright grumpiness. But I haven't had to even work on my own cheerful state, and every day Yuri has given his gloomy weather report, I've felt a new surge of relief. Here I am trapped, and I feel absolutely no impulse to escape. How can this be?

Then a couple days ago it dawned on me: Who says I'm trapped? Granted, I may be stuck in Provideniya, but for the first time since I can remember, I feel free—from deadlines, from expectations, from the compulsion to keep strategizing an end to my dry spell. Everything I dreaded has since passed—the New Millennium, the wedding, the One Thousand Days. There are no loose-cannon grandparents around to torment me and no Internet matchmaking services to consume me, and certainly there aren't any other dating opportunities.

In case you're curious, neither Yuri nor Don, the computer guy, has any spark potential—and that's probably a good thing, considering I ran out of my birth control pills yesterday. Besides that, where does anybody go for a date around here? The nearest Starbucks must be a thousand miles away.

Right now, there's not one damn thing I can do about the Streak, and it's marvelous. Maybe this is how it feels to be a kid in Duluth when a blizzard shuts down school. I'm in the middle of one long, protracted "snow day."

I have, as you're aware, been trying to use this opportunity to make some sense of the Streak, to finally get to the bottom of my single state. And, finally, I think, I'm figuring a few things out.

For starters, even though I've had enough bad dates to last two lifetimes, I'm not sure I can lay the blame for the Streak on my pile of rejects. Now, with the luxury of distance, I have to admit that the majority of the guys I've been out with over the past three years have been decent-enough fellows. The philandering philosophy professor notwithstanding, most had the basic requisites—agreeable personalities, pleasant appearances, good manners, and the ability to make direct eye contact. In fact, I probably gave up three reasonable chances at breaking the Streak when I dismissed those three guys a few weeks back for lack of sparkness.

So why'd I do it? Good question. I guess it's because I didn't consider them Streak-breaking material. Which is odd, because haven't I always assumed I'd be happy to bed down with Mr. Remote Possibility?

Honestly, if the Streak has bothered me as much as it has, why haven't I just taken the path of least resistance and put an end to it? I mean, it's not that hard to find sex. Surely I could have just marched myself over to the nearest singles' bar and made my intentions known. Last month I had a guy wanting to pay me to have sex, didn't I?

But hold on, are you seeing what I think I'm seeing? Somewhere along the way—who knows when—I began to do exactly what I thought I was incapable of doing. I began to . . . *hold out*. This couldn't have been conscious, of course. But I do know that, for the past year or so, I've been gauging each date against one standard and one standard alone: Is he the right one to break the Streak? I'm always thinking, *If I've been waiting this long, it better damn well be worth it.* Isn't that rich? I'm thirty-four years old and I've regressed to the virginal mindset of "saving myself"— a mindset, I should add, that I don't remember possessing even as a virgin.

Could it be? Despite all my preoccupation with sex, have I actually grown *protective* of the Streak?

This certainly puts a whole new spin on things. Granted, I've never felt the Streak was entirely about sex; but is the Streak not about sex at all? Now that I know I've been eliminating the remote possibilities, maybe what I really have been looking for—all along—is Mr. Some Measure of Probability.

But what now? Could this strategy be dooming me to failure? What if I keep waiting and waiting and the Streak-breaker never shows up?

I think that's exactly what Ann, the cabinet member who has always struck me as so wise, was trying to get at shortly before I left for Fairbanks. She told me a story that left me unsettled even though I couldn't explain why. It was a Buddhist parable about a woman being chased by tigers: The woman falls over a cliff and manages to grasp a slippery vine. Tigers above, the abyss below, clinging to life, she plucks a strawberry from the vine and eats it with great relish.

"You need to become a Buddhist right away!" Ann said. "It's all wrong to be postponing your happiness until you fulfill certain conditions. Everyone has some version of that: 'If only I had X, I'd be happy.' 'If only I were ten years younger I'd be happy.' But the truth is, anyone—single women included—can be happy. This doesn't mean you shouldn't keep looking for the right guy, but why wait for something that may not even bring you what you want when you could savor today?"

The advice seemed so sensible at the time that I didn't see how I could argue against it. But a week in Nina's apartment has somehow given me a new vantage point. Haven't I already tested out the strawberry-relishing philosophy? Surely that's what my three years with Alec were all about. And in the end, I discovered it wasn't enough.

And let's face it: The woman in the Buddhist parable knew her prospects were dim. The strawberry was all she had going on. Personally, I've been operating on the assumption that I've got more options. Sure, my clock is ticking, but age thirty-four is hardly the time to throw in the towel and start shopping for the stretch pants and Winnebago.

Maybe it's just the thrill of my arm-wrestling victory or the odd high I've gotten from being stranded, but despite everything, I'm feeling remarkably optimistic. I know the impossible can happen, because it already has. A thousand-odd days ago I couldn't imagine going so long without sex, but here I've done it. Call me nuts, but in some strange, convoluted way, that gives me hope. I will find my Streakbreaker. Or he will find me. Whatever. He's out there, and someday we're going to have endless, steamy, worth-the-wait sex.

In the meantime, I'll just relax and enjoy Provideniya. My bed is comfy, and Nina whips up these really tasty crepelike pancakes. The other day, I made flashcards of the Russian alphabet from my *Lonely Planet* book, and Yuri has promised to teach me the proper pronunciation. Who knows—we may be stranded long enough for me to read *War and Peace* as Tolstoy wrote it. Scrabble is still going strong. Yesterday, in response to complaints about low scores, I penciled in four new Double Word Score boxes on the board, boosting morale considerably. I'd say I'm being plenty productive, and I'm putting my energy to good use.

I'm not sure I can say the same for our resident grumps, Don and Jim. Not content to make the best of our little life here and wait for the airport to open, they have spent countless hours concocting the craziest schemes to get us out of here—plans that are as loony, if you ask me, as anything Gilligan and his fellow castaways ever drummed up.

The other day, for example, Don became obsessed with the idea of having us evacuated by helicopter to St. Lawrence Island, the closest U.S. territory, something like forty miles away. It's all he could talk about for hours. He became so excited by this plan that he begged Yuri to find him a phone so he could call the president of Bering Air, our Nome-based charter company. An hour or so later, Don came back with his head hanging. We could only be rescued by helicopter, he reported, if we had a life-or-death medical emergency, in which case Bering Air would contact the U.S. State

Department, which would then dispatch a Black Hawk for the rescue. Don agreed, reluctantly, that our little predicament does not warrant intervention from Colin Powell.

Then Jim came up with an alternative plan: chartering a boat from Nome to come save us. Jim and Don trudged back to the borrowed phone for another call to the president of Bering Air. The upshot: another big, fat *nyet*. Turns out that (1) there are no boats in Nome that can safely cross the Bering Strait, and (2) even if there were, it would take at least five weeks to get permission from the Russian government to come ashore.

Still, Jim and Don forged on. Another scheme involved boarding a German cruise ship that is rumored to be docking in Provideniya for a few hours sometime this week. (I have no clue how rumors have floated into Nina's third-floor apartment.) But even Don backed off from this idea when I pointed out that we have no idea *where the ship is going*. What if it's headed for Japan?

Hands down, their most creative plan was the one they cooked up the one day that Provideniya was actually clear enough for our plane to take off but—much to our shock—Nome wasn't clear enough for a landing. The plan was to get back to Nome "the other way"; in other words, Provideniya to Anadyr (the next city over) to Moscow, then just a hop, skip and a jump to London, New York, Seattle, Anchorage, and Nome.

A couple hours ago I snapped at them to get over it and come play some Scrabble. But they were too deep into their latest plot—something to do with getting the Russian government to deport us. Honestly, I haven't heard anything so ridiculous since . . . since . . . Wait. Holy shit. Since . . . *me*.

I mean, really . . . Lollapasuza? Feng shui? Speed

Dating? Running off to Bend? Sending the letter to the red-haired guy at the SEC? Profiling match.com prospects as if they were on the FBI's Ten Most Wanted list? Am I really any different from Jim and Don? And what about all my escape schemes? Winnemucca, Nairobi, Jackpot, Reykjavík, Mission: Implausible . . . Provideniya! What in the hell have I been thinking?

Jim, Don . . . and me. The Three Stooges. All of us frantically trying to come up with some way, *any* way to get out of our respective predicaments . . . and getting nowhere.

For days, I've been dishing out advice to Moe and Curly over there: Mellow out. Relax. Stop trying so hard. And look at me. . . . Practically since the day I broke up with Alec, I've never truly let up. Maybe it's time to stop treating my personal quest a little less like the battle plan for the D-Day invasion. Maybe, as I keep telling Don and Jim, there are some things in life that you just can't make happen. Maybe all you can do is be ready.

Well, I guess it's pretty obvious what I need to do now. I've got to stop all my strategizing and find a way to lighten up. But how do I do that without feeling like I'm giving up? And how can I possibly do it now that the Streak has grown to such colossal proportions? I can't just whisk it away.

Or can I?

I've always operated under the assumption that there's only one way to end this dry spell, and it has to involve a penis. But maybe I need to do a little more creative thinking here. I'm the one—aren't I?—who created this behemoth. I'm the one who knows exactly when the Streak started, so I'm the only one who can really keep the tally going—or not.

I wonder: If you go without sex for over a thousand

days and no one is there to count it, does it still make a streak?

All my friends kept insisting I forget about my thousand-day milestone, but maybe they didn't go far enough. If I can't break the Streak between the sheets, then why not just ignore it into oblivion?

That's it! Enough with the Streak. Bye-bye. *Adios.* Or, as they say here in Russia, *Da svidaniya!*

And what a fitting time to say good-bye. A few moments ago, Yuri stopped to tell us the airport has finally reopened, and all's clear in Nome. We're due to take off in about an hour.

I guess I won't be staying another month after all. Ah, well. I'd better go pack up my things. The Scrabble board is definitely coming with me, and so is the *Gilligan's Island* song sheet. I want to see how well my memory served me.

Oh, and I've been rambling so much I forgot to mention: When Yuri came with his news, he also brought me the printout of an e-mail from my sister. A few days ago, he arranged for me to send a message via one of the few people in town with Internet access. I could only send one, and instinct told me to send it to Jen. "Tell everyone I'm stuck here but totally fine," I wrote. "And pls. tape *Law & Order.*"

Jen wrote back that she hoped I'd be home soon and that she was relieved I was safe. I'm relieved, too, that the Cold War appears to be thawing. (And how appropriate that I'm in Russia!)

I just glanced out the window and saw for myself that the fog has lifted. For the first time in days—or, come to think of it, maybe years—I can really see what's out there.

EPILOGUE

The Age of Enlightenment

Sex is a short cut to everything.

—Anne Cumming

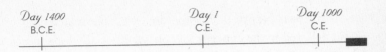

23

Grandma Gets the Last Word

*Y*es, yes, I broke the Streak. You never had any doubt, did you?

I'll tell you all about it, but before I do, let's rewind to a moment eight months after my liberation from Provideniya, when I was having lunch at a Mexican restaurant with Allan, my lone male cabinet member. "So," he said to me, "it's a good thing you're not trying to date right now since your scalp is flaking off into your burrito."

At this point the Streak was still technically alive—not that I was counting! But I had more pressing concerns, like the fact that (1) my foot was in a cast, (2) my arm was in a sling, and (3) I had developed a raging case of psoriasis, which meant any little shake of my head created a kind of snow-globe effect. Allan had a point. If I'd shown up on a coffee date, no matter what percentage of my charm I turned on, any guy would have bolted for the nearest exit.

In the post-Provideniya months, I had more or less kept my vow to stop trying so hard. Soon after my return, I'd decided it was best to take some time off from match.com. I still believed in the concept, of course, especially for someone like me who worked alone at home in pajamas and a towel turban. But I knew if I was truly going to find a different pace, I was going to have to coast for a while. For the time being, I figured *que sera, sera,* and I'd channel my energies instead into training for the bike-racing season. Who knows if I could have maintained my more laid-back state any longer than a few months, because unforeseen circumstances soon started doing the job for me.

Fluke nerve damage in my shoulder and the worsening of a longtime foot injury forced me to undergo two separate surgeries just two weeks apart. In the midst of it all, the psoriasis emerged, proving so stubborn that not even the highest dosage of drugs—"enough to kill a small elephant," as my dermatologist put it—was having any impact.

Nancy accused me of fabricating my medical problems to forget about my dry spell. "Now you've developed Munchausen's syndrome?" she asked one day.

I denied the allegation, of course. Even at my looniest, I did have my limits. But I will concede that, as in Provideniya, it was a relief to be in a position where circumstances were truly out of my control. After all, you can't do much but just "let things happen" when you're under general anesthesia. Being flat on your back with your leg elevated and foot encased in an ice-filled bootie is pretty conducive to mellowing out, too.

My initial recuperation occurred at my parents' house, and every few days Allan was kind enough to come over and spring me for lunch. It had been a brutal recovery, not because of any physical pain—both operations went beautifully and caused minimal discomfort—but because the TV in my parents' guest bedroom was barely functional. Worse, my parents didn't have TiVo, the ingenious digital-recording device I'd just acquired that enables you to stockpile hours upon hours of programming essentially at the touch of a button. While my new gizmo sat lonely and neglected back at my condo, I was now at the mercy of the daytime TV schedule.

Eventually my foot and shoulder healed, my psoriasis subsided, and I returned to the comfort of my condo and my TiVo. I finally felt ready and eager for a fresh start, and that meant one thing—reactivating Fitwriter, my match.com handle. This time around, though, signing up felt different. The urgency seemed to have faded.

My first night back on the system, I took a relaxed scroll through the profiles, resisting the impulse to deconstruct and instead watching and waiting for a gut feeling. Eventually, one guy caught my eye—a boyishly handsome, thirty-four-year-old redhead who called himself Outdoor-Runner. (I'd never realized it before the SEC guy, but I did seem to have a certain weakness for red hair.) "Run away with me!" was his corny subtitle. Not that mine, "*Law & Order* addict," was any less goofy.

His profile was succinct and straightforward and, for the most part, unremarkable. The activities he enjoyed—running, cycling, yoga, hiking, diving—offered an important prerequisite, but then, there were plenty of athletic guys in match.comland. Two things about OutdoorRunner, however, did stand out. First, in the description of his "ideal match," he had resisted the "petite, slender, preferably blond" mantra that was so common on the system. In fact, nowhere did he mention any physical attributes he was looking for—surprising, in my experience, for a guy who looked to be so cute. What he was seeking, he wrote, was a

"woman who is intelligent, humorous, sincere, and loving." Which brings me to the second refreshing feature of
his profile: He used the word "loving" not just there but in
two more places. Here, I suspected, was a guy eminently
capable of using the term "I feel" in a sentence other than
"I feel like eating at Burger King."

I decided to go with my gut feeling, which was that I
liked this guy.

He responded to my e-mail right away. "I love *Law &
Order,* too!" he wrote. I decided not to read too much into
that, but I did feel encouraged when he suggested meeting
for coffee the next day. I'd found a predate kind of guy! We
arranged to meet at a local coffee joint, since my usual
Starbucks was too crowded on Sundays.

With his thick red hair, he was easy to spot standing
in the order line. Wearing a marathon T-shirt, khaki
shorts, and sandals, he was even cuter than his picture—
tall and lean, with strong hands, deep blue eyes, and an
easy smile. "You're Paul!" I said, marveling at my good
fortune.

Within moments after we sat down, I could feel a
spark. Our conversation flowed easily from topic to topic—
his running races, my bike races, his year in Iowa, my year
in Bend—and he laughed at my best lines. He had a few,
too. He briefly explained his job as a software engineer in
aerospace—something about commercial jets and "datalink
systems"—and then he added, to my relief, "If I tell you
any more, your eyes will glaze over. So when's your next
bike race?" We talked for almost two hours, which was
about an hour and a half longer than my average predate.
I ended our afternoon together by giving him my phone
number and telling him that I hoped he'd call.

Walking to my car, I caught myself thinking, for the first time since the philandering philosopher: *Maybe I've found the Streak-breaker!* But this time, I didn't have to poke around to find something intriguing about the guy. This time I thought, *Everything's intriguing.*

Paul called the next day, and I happily accepted a dinner invitation for Chinese. But even with the spark, I still tempered my expectations. When you're in a drought like the one I had going, you just don't get too fluttery before a second date.

Now, here's where the story veers off course a bit. On our second date, the spark just vanished. Poof. History. I had no idea where it went, and even worse, I didn't know what to do. In all my discussions about sparkness, I'd never covered the issue of intermittent sparkness. If it goes out, can it ever come back?

Gamely, I kept working at our conversation, but it just seemed to drag. So I resorted to the one topic I knew I could generate boundless enthusiasm for: TiVo.

In the few months since I'd gotten TiVo, I'd become such a convert that I found myself compulsively evangelizing, trying to explain to the uninitiated that it was far more than just a souped-up VCR. As Paul and I ate our lettuce wraps, I launched into a sermonette about the miracle of TiVo—about recording any show's entire season at the touch of the "Season Pass" button, about recording two programs at once, about zipping through commercials, about pausing live TV.

"I'm no longer a slave to the networks' TV schedule!" I bubbled. "I've been freed!"

I've had all kinds of reactions to my TiVo testimonials, but no one has ever—before or since—responded the way Paul did.

"How big is the hard drive?" he asked. And: "Which digital format does TiVo use?"

Aside from the fact that I couldn't begin to answer these questions, I felt he was missing the point. This was like discussing the brilliance of Monet's *Water Lilies* and asking, "What brand of paint do you think he used?"

I'd never imagined myself with an engineering type, and at that moment, I still couldn't. The date ended with a decidedly unsexy hug, and I no longer thought Paul was my go-to guy. That night I reported to Margie that, even with my TiVo riff, I'd used only forty percent of my charm.

"I'll give it one more chance if he wants to," I said, "but I don't think I'll be too disappointed if he doesn't."

The next morning Paul e-mailed to say he'd had a great time. "I'm sold—when do I get my TiVo demo?" he asked. Hmmm. Suddenly he was speaking my language again.

The moment I saw him on the next date—the red hair, the blue eyes, the sweet smile—the spark was back. Just like that. Even without my trying to bring it back, even after I'd decided it was gone for good.

Our conversation flowed easily over pizza; then we went to my place. I showed off my TiVo, and he responded with sufficiently enthusiastic "oohs" and "aahs." I could easily have ended the Streak that night. (Paul later admitted he would have been game, too.) But I didn't. Instead, around midnight, I stood up and sort of escorted him to the door, leaving him with just a short kiss on the lips.

Yes, it's true—I was holding out. But only because I thought it would be ill-mannered to give in to my overwhelming impulse, which was to pounce on the poor boy right then and there. Besides, I still wanted to make doubly sure we were heading in the same direction.

That night I barely slept. All I could think about was Paul and sex—and sex with Paul. The next morning I e-mailed him at work. "I just want to make sure you didn't get the wrong idea last night," I told him. "I was afraid that if we'd had a real kiss, I wouldn't have been able to stop. It's been a long time—longer than you could possibly fathom." I hadn't been so boldly flirtatious since BikeMan, and I nervously awaited his reply.

It arrived quickly. "I must admit," he wrote, "when I got home I lay awake a little while thinking of where that kiss could have led. It's good to know we are thinking along the same lines."

At that moment I knew. My wait was over. The Streak was going to end.

Now you might think, given my sexual deficit level, that this realization would have been shortly followed by shrieks of joy and copious tears. You might think I'd have been anxious, even frantic for what was now certain to happen. But I wasn't. All I felt was calm and confident and happy. The Streak was going to be over, but not out of desperation or exhaustion or wishful thinking. Paul wasn't something I'd conjured up out of cyberspace, like BikeMan. This was for real.

For the first time in forever—and for the last time ever—I went to the calendar, flipped through the months, and calculated the Streak. But it seemed almost irrelevant. This wasn't about having sex. This was about having sex with Paul.

Two nights later, on a Saturday after an Indian dinner that we both rushed through but pretended we didn't, I invited him back to my condo with one thing in mind. But as soon as we walked into my living room, he sat down on the couch and said, "Want to watch some TiVo?"

TiVo????

I sat down next to him and took his hand.

"No, um, TiVo isn't really what I had in mind," I said as I kissed him. "Let's go to my guest bedroom."

"Oh, I think we could stay right here for a while," he said.

Geez, was this guy dense or just exceedingly polite? (He later admitted he was just being polite.)

"No, *really*," I said, more as a command than a suggestion. "LET'S GO TO MY GUEST BEDROOM."

Before he knew what was happening, I'd grabbed his hand and was leading him down the hallway. As for the sex, ah well . . . Let's just say it was definitely of the worth-the-wait variety, and leave the rest to your imagination. Afterward, I remember feeling so comfortable and happy in his arms and realizing that all my worries had been unfounded, that sex was even easier than riding a bike. It was as easy as taking my next breath.

What I recall most vividly about that entire sleepless night was Paul's reaction, a few hours later, when I told him about the Streak.

I'd wrestled with whether I should reveal my big secret, knowing well it was the sort of information that could send certain guys sprinting out the door. But I had so much confidence that Paul wasn't one of those guys that I decided to take the chance. Besides, it was too good a story *not* to tell. We were still in bed when I offered him the condensed version. Once I was done, he looked at me in shock and said simply, "ONE THOUSAND THREE HUNDRED AND FIFTY-EIGHT DAYS?"

"Yeah, I know," I said. "It's kind of hard to grasp."

It seemed like five minutes before he was able to speak again. "But . . . but . . . you're so *normal*. How could that be?"

I think it's the sweetest thing anyone has ever said to me.

Our date lasted the rest of the weekend. At one point, Paul admitted that when I originally told him, in my e-mail, that it had been a "long time" since I'd had sex, he thought I meant four, maybe six months. I had to laugh. "Man, I could do six months standing on my head!" I told him, sounding like a career criminal on *Law & Order*.

When Paul finally left for work Monday morning, I rushed to the phone to report to my friends the startling new developments. They were, of course, thrilled. And not just for me.

"I didn't really want to tell you this," Nancy said, "but I was at the end of my rope. I can't ever live through something like this again! Tell Paul, *thank you.*"

"Don't wear the poor guy out," Allan said. "Remember, you don't have to make up for it all at once."

The first month was incredible. We were like human suction cups, as Alec and I had been, except without the red flags. My friends worried that I might be confusing my feelings for Paul with the excitement of ending the Streak, but I never once thought so. Whether we were in bed or not, I just loved being with him, and everything Paul said and did told me he felt the same way.

When I think about why something so right finally happened, there is, of course, only one explanation: It was luck. In a big, huge way. I was lucky I saw Paul's profile and lucky he responded to mine and lucky that he e-mailed me for a third date when I was perfectly willing to let him go. For all my years of trying, what I realized in Provideniya turned out to be right. Life really is a combination of what you make happen and what happens to you. You just have to be ready.

It's entirely possible that I could have tried match.com for four more years and 150 more dates and still gotten nowhere. But then, too, if I hadn't tried at all, I never would have met Paul.

Everything was going so well that after a month and a half I felt secure enough to take the next step: It was time to introduce Paul to my family. I evaluated the calendar of family get-togethers and settled on Grandma Honey's ninety-first birthday dinner, figuring there would be enough people—about a dozen—and enough commotion to keep Paul from feeling like a suspect in an interrogation room.

At this point, I hadn't offered up a whole lot of information to Paul about my family. I'd learned from the introduction of previous boyfriends that no amount of explaining fully prepares you for the Schlosberg family experience, and it's better to simply go in cold, without any preconceived notions or worries.

I wasn't a bit concerned about what my family would think of Paul. How could anyone not adore him? Besides, being a living, breathing male under age forty was certainly enough to trigger a spontaneous ecstatic reaction among them. However, I will admit that once or twice I considered suggesting to Paul a certain attire for the party, given my family's kooky definition of "appropriately dressed" and the fact that you only get to make a first impression once. On the other hand, I didn't want to seem overbearing or increase Paul's anxiety level, so I decided against offering any hints. I just crossed my fingers and hoped.

Ah, wishful thinking. Paul slept at my place the night before the birthday dinner, and when I saw how he dressed for work the next morning, I had this sinking feeling. He'd selected perhaps his most quintessential software-engineer-in-a-cubicle shirt—a dark plaid button-down with short sleeves.

Immediately, I flashed back to an incident known among some in my family as the Short-Sleeved Disaster. This had occurred a couple years before when my cousin's husband showed up for a family dinner wearing a short-sleeved shirt. Grandpa, who had on a sportcoat, was so furious he was practically spitting.

"Everyone in their right mind knows how to dress for dinner!" he bellowed, leaving the poor guy stunned and speechless for the rest of the evening.

That's really not what I had in mind for the introductory meeting between my family and my first boyfriend in nearly five years. But what could I do? Paul lived too far away to go home and pick up a dress shirt before the dinner, and he was already a little nervous about meeting my family, even without explicit knowledge of their eccentricities. So I knew I was in a quandary. But before I could figure out how to fix the problem, or whether to even mention that we had one, Paul was out the door.

By early afternoon, my mild unease had blossomed into full-fledged anxiety, and I called my cousin for advice.

"Go to Banana Republic *right now,*" she said, reminding me of the Short-Sleeved Disaster. "Don't take any chances. It's just not worth it."

Then I called Jen, who thankfully was speaking to me again. The turning point had come six months earlier as my mother was making a speech at a family Chanukah party. I have no recollection of what she said, but it was aggravating enough that my sister and I, sitting at opposite sides of the room, simultaneously blurted out, *"Mother!"* We glanced at each other and rolled our eyes and had been on the road to reconciliation ever since.

My sister was even more emphatic than my cousin on the shirt issue. "Go to Banana Republic and buy *two* shirts," she said. "That way you can at least let him choose."

To get the male perspective on this predicament, and to make sure the rest of us weren't overreacting, I called my sister's husband on his cell phone in New York City, where he was auditioning for a part. "Oh my God, get him a dress shirt *for sure*," he said. "And I highly recommend you speak to your father."

John went on to reveal his dressing strategy for our family occasions. "First I find out what your father is wearing," he explained, "and then I go up one level. Like, if he's wearing a dress shirt, I wear a tie. If he's wearing a tie, I wear a suit. I always have to go up one notch since his clothes are nicer."

I decided against involving my father in this mess, but at least I had my answer: I had to take action. And fast. At this point, dinner was barely an hour away. I called Paul to give him the heads-up.

"Okay, what I'm about to tell you is completely ridiculous and it's absolutely no reflection on you. Please keep in mind that my family is insane. Now that that's settled, would it be okay if I went over to Banana Republic and bought a dress shirt for you to wear to dinner?"

Silence.

"Um, no, that's not really okay. What I'm wearing is fine."

"*Please* don't take this personally. It has nothing whatsoever to do with you. It's my family—like I said, they're insane. But seriously, things will go a lot better tonight if I just run out and pick you up a long-sleeved shirt."

"What are you talking about? My shirt is perfectly fine. It's summer. It's hot. Short sleeves are fine."

Obviously, he was not grasping the enormity of the crisis. After several more tense exchanges, Paul finally, reluctantly, relented.

"I promise—this is for your own protection," I said.

"Whatever," he said.

I sped to the mall, dashed into Banana Republic, and announced to the first saleswoman in sight, "I have an emergency! My new boyfriend is about to meet my family and I need two dress shirts *right now.* What goes with red hair?"

The saleswoman picked out a pale green shirt and a light blue shirt. I paid for them, then flew to Paul's office. As he opened my car door, he was shaking his head, looking like a man who was about to be dressed by his mother.

"I *cannot* believe you did this," he said. "This is totally ridiculous."

"Yeah, but look at it this way—you're getting a free shirt out of it! Which one do you want to wear?"

He chose the blue one. We drove on in silence.

When we arrived at the party, held in a private room of my grandparents' retirement home, my first priority, of course, was to scope out what the other men had on. Sure enough, they were wearing sportcoats or suits. I knew I'd made the right call for Paul. It may have caused our first fight, but at least we'd dodged the bullet!

My family was on their best behavior as I introduced Paul around in the lobby. To my great relief, it was nothing like when the little space aliens swarmed Richard Dreyfuss at the end of *Close Encounters*. I could tell from their smiles and their jokes that my family liked him. Things proceeded nicely, with comfortable small talk as we sat down for dinner.

Then, about a half hour into the meal, I looked over at Paul, who was seated to my right, and my jaw dropped. Between his nerves, the long sleeves, and the warm room, he'd broken into a full-fledged flop sweat. Dozens of tiny sweat droplets were balanced on his forehead and nose. His hair, now sopping wet, had turned a deep shade of orange. And the brand-new shirt was drenched, as if he'd been caught in a downpour without an umbrella.

Paul looked at me helplessly and whispered, "What should I *do*?"

I whispered back, "The bathroom?"

A few minutes later he mustered the courage to excuse himself and head off to the restroom. The whole time I was in a panic, certain he was cursing me for making him wear the long sleeves. He stayed gone so long, it fleetingly crossed my mind that he may have just kept walking, and I wasn't sure I would have blamed him.

Finally, he reappeared, his shirt still sopping wet, but at least his face was dry. And he didn't look mad at all. In fact, he just looked at me, smiled, and shrugged.

I knew all was well. In so many ways, besides the evening.

As we finished our desserts, Grandma Honey stood to make her speech. After she thanked my father for the flowers and said a few more words—actually, more than a few—she looked in our direction. *Oh, no,* I thought. *Here we go. What's she going to say this time?*

"I want to welcome Paul to this family occasion," she began. "I know that Suzanne wouldn't have brought him here if he wasn't a special fellow."

For once, Grandma Honey got it right.

About the Author

Suzanne Schlosberg's humor and travel writing has appeared in the *Los Angeles Times, Shape,* and *Sand in My Bra: Funny Women Write from the Road,* among other publications. Suzanne is the author and coauthor of several fitness books, including *Fitness for Dummies, Weight Training for Dummies,* and *Fitness for Travelers.* She lives in Los Angeles with her husband, Paul Spencer.

Suzanne can be reached through her Web site: suzanneschlosberg.com.